Praise for
The Naked Gospel

How do you know a sailboat is maxed out in the wind? The author's wife, a sailboat captain, can tell you. It hydroplanes. How do you know it's hydroplaning? You listen for the hum. This book shows you how to open the sails of your life to the winds of truth and max out in God's Spirit. Read this book and hear the hum.

—LEONARD SWEET,
bestselling author of *So Beautiful:
Divine Design for Life and the Church*

Our culture screams at us, "Productivity!"—and often, this mantra gets absorbed and spread by the church. *Grace* is a word we use often but rarely understand the depth and true meaning of. In *The Naked Gospel*, Andrew Farley strips down religion and shows us the faith and freedom God intends for us to have in a fully abundant, radiant life.

—ANNE JACKSON,
speaker and author of *Mad Church Disease*

What a great "textbook" on how to strip away all the religious fakery and take the challenge to just be a normal person while being a healthy Christian.

—STEVE ARTERBURN,
founder and chairman
of New Life Ministries

Reading Andrew Farley's book *The Naked Gospel* harkened me back to my own faith-altering encounter with Jesus when I first embraced the outrageous idea of the exchanged life. That message dynamically changed me, which is why I'm excited about Andrew's book—a biblically centered freedom manual for today's stuck Christian. If you're tired of wearing the "I'm a super Christian" mask, if you're weary and discouraged on the inside, read this book and experience the freedom Jesus brings.

—MARY DEMUTH,
author of *Daisy Chain*

The Naked Gospel is an intelligently written book that is thoroughly intriguing. Your church or small group could benefit greatly by its wisdom and concepts. This is a must-read!

—DAVE STONE,
senior minister,
Southeast Christian Church

The message that Andrew Farley brings in *The Naked Gospel* is so necessary for the church today. It is absolutely essential for a fulfilling and genuinely Christ-centered life.

—JOHN BEST, ThD,
former professor of New Testament
Literature and Exegesis,
Dallas Theological Seminary

For over three years, I have co-hosted radio and television programs with Dr. Andrew Farley. God has gifted this insightful teacher and author with the ability to communicate the meaning of the Scriptures with remarkable simplicity. The clarity of his words should refresh the spirit of every saint and beckon to the lost. The heart of his message is captured here, and it comes at the perfect time, when the United States, and indeed the whole world, is hungering for answers. *The Naked Gospel* is unabashed truth.

—CHIP POLK,
cofounder and playwright,
Ragtown Gospel Theater

the naked
GOSPEL

the naked
GOSPEL

the truth you may never hear in church

Andrew Farley

ZONDERVAN®

ZONDERVAN.com/
AUTHORTRACKER
follow your favorite authors

ZONDERVAN

The Naked Gospel
Copyright © 2009 by Andrew Farley

This title is also available as a Zondervan ebook. Visit www.zondervan.com/ebooks.

This title is also available in a Zondervan audio edition. Visit www.zondervan.fm.

Requests for information should be addressed to:

Zondervan, *Grand Rapids, Michigan 49530*

Library of Congress Cataloging-in-Publication Data

Farley, Andrew, 1972-
    The naked gospel : the truth you may never hear in church / Andrew Farley.
        p.   cm.
    Includes bibliographical references.
    ISBN 978-0-310-29306-4 (softcover)
    1. Christian life. 2. Theology, Doctrinal — Popular works. I. Title.
    BV4501.3.F36   2009
    230 — dc22   2008054098

Published in association with the literary agency of Alive Communications, Inc., 7680 Goddard Street, Suite 200, Colorado Springs, CO 80920. www.alivecommunications.com

Interior design by Beth Shagene

Printed in the United States of America

---

09 10 11 12 13 14 • 25 24 23 22 21 20 19 18 17 16 15 14 13 12 11 10 9 8 7 6 5 4 3

For my son, Gavin—a map.
Yeah, it's *really* this good.
It's even better than I could explain.
Enjoy the New, and enjoy Him!
I'm proud of you, boy.

contents

fair warning • 15

*The naked gospel [is] discovering what was the gospel
which our Lord and his apostles preached; what additions
and alterations latter ages have made in it;
what advantages and damages have thereupon ensued.*

Arthur Bury, 1691

Arthur Bury's book titled *The Naked Gospel*
was burned by the church of his day.

fair warning

THE REAL, NAKED GOSPEL IS A LOT BETTER THAN ANY OF US REALIZE. A word of warning, though: You might throw this book down in disgust; you might pick it back up again in curiosity; you might shake your head in frustration as you wonder, "How could I have missed this before?" or "Is this guy crazy?"

When it comes to Christianity, I realize it's more palatable to talk in generalities. It's risky to draw lines in the sand and confront disagreements. But you may have noticed that much of the New Testament was written to correct misunderstandings and false doctrine. Apparently, pushing absolutes and even splitting theological hairs are supposed to be part of healthy church life.

Christians today are grateful for Jesus and heaven. Some of us go to church every time the doors are open. Some listen to hundreds of sermons each year. Some memorize scores of Bible verses. Some even hold a few degrees in God stuff.

Despite all of our fervor, many of us are still apathetic instead of ecstatic over the gospel. But maybe there's an answer to our heartfelt yearning for more passion in our Christian life.

Is *this* kind of Christianity—the kind that replaces apathy with ecstasy—too good to be true? Actually, I believe it's the only kind that's biblical. However, it seems that today it's the truth you may never hear in church.

> We find too much fluff, double-talk, misleading jargon, and pat answers in many churches today.

We find too much fluff, double-talk, misleading jargon, and pat answers in many churches today. No matter how much you hear it or how much it entertains you, it won't bring genuine and enduring fulfillment. There's only one message that I've found to bring real and lasting change. It's the *naked* gospel.

AN INVITATION

I once thought I knew all about the Christian faith, but it wasn't until fourteen years after I'd received Christ that I would begin to grasp the real thing. I'm not talking about another salvation experience or a second blessing. I'm talking about a return to the foot of the cross and the door of the tomb to learn all over again.

And for me, there was as much *un*learning as learning.

With that in mind, I invite you to dive deeply with me toward the indispensable, powerful core of the Christian faith. I found genuine answers that don't disappoint. I'm excited to share them with you. I'm betting you'll be surprised at least a time or two along the way.

The real thing has a tendency to do that.

PART 1

obsessive-Christianity disorder

We may spend our days in what we call our religious duties,
and we may fill our devotions with fervor, and still may be miserable.
Nothing can set our hearts at rest but a real acquaintance with God.

Hannah Whitall Smith (1832–1911)

1

MEDS, THERAPY, AND A MENTAL HEALTH FACILITY—THESE WERE the solutions I was offered. One counselor suggested that my condition wouldn't change for the rest of my life and that I'd always need medication. As desperate as I was, I just didn't buy it. There had to be some other answer to my problem. After trying several Christian therapists, each of whom employed a different approach, no one could alter the patterned behaviors I was stuck in.

After all, obsessive Bible study and street evangelism aren't your run-of-the-mill symptoms.

MY BEGINNING

In high school, I was popular, earned good grades, and was elected president of the student body. I had no trouble making friends and making friends laugh. I enjoyed success in sports, in theatre, and with girls. None of these areas contributed to the deep-seated inferiority that I felt.

The trouble for me was that I didn't seem to stack up in another arena—the *spiritual* one. Whether it was the church, my Christian high school, Christian camps, or even Christian concerts I attended, they all implied the same thing: you need to rededicate, recommit, and be different. You're not doing enough.

Don't be satisfied. Don't be stagnant. Never rest. There's *always* more to do for God.

Fear. Guilt. Pressure. These were the motivators that hooked me early on and nearly killed me. Killed me? Yeah, I had close encounters with death or serious injury a few times. I took a two-by-four to the head once in a dangerous neighborhood while street evangelizing. Another time, I was thrown to the pavement by a drug dealer whom I was trying to convert.

Committed? You bet. But committed to what? Although I'd stand up on the subway and preach to the entire train car, I was still empty inside. Despite my willingness to go door-to-door witnessing in my own neighborhood, I really had no life of fulfillment to offer. Whether I was preaching on a train, in neighborhoods, or even in the local jail, there was always an underlying anxiety.

> Although I'd stand up on the subway and preach to the entire train car, I was still empty inside.

I grew up with a flavor of the gospel that assured me I was going to heaven, but that didn't help with the present turmoil. I was afraid God was so thoroughly disappointed with my performance that he wouldn't use me, grow me, or "have fellowship" with me. Voices around me only confirmed that I was falling short and needed to strive yet again to meet the standard.

You wouldn't have known any of this bothered me, because I never let it show. But after years of not being considered for the Christian Character Award at school, it got to me. The key to winning the award was to be quiet or even shy. Those who didn't say much at all were labeled "meek." The problem for me was that my personality didn't fit the requirements.

I had a personal relationship with Christ. I knew my Bible better than many. And I really cared about my friends at school. But I was the class clown and the life of the party. Humor and Christian character just didn't mix.

MY MIDDLE

"I'll be different in college," I told myself. This was my opportunity to change—to find a whole new environment and start with a clean slate. I received acceptance letters from two universities. One was Wheaton College, perhaps the best Christian college in the nation; the other was Furman University, a reputable school in the South. After informing my parents that I wasn't "a good enough Christian to study at Wheaton," I accepted the invitation to study at Furman.

My first year at Furman was a transition. I decided I no longer wanted to be mediocre in the spiritual arena. I wanted to earn the respect of God and of those around me. After poring over dozens of Christian books, I felt more knowledgeable than most of my peers. I delivered my first church sermon at the age of nineteen. I evangelized on the streets in Spain, Greece, and Italy while on study-abroad trips. I was intense, and everyone around me knew it.

After I returned to the United States, I lost all my friends. Who could blame them? I had changed. I still remember one of my best friends telling another friend that he was embarrassed to be seen with me.

Sure, some outsiders applauded me and respected me. But they were strangers. All they saw was the product—some were coming to faith in Christ, and others appeared to benefit from my "discipleship." But these were the minority. Most could detect that there was something not right within me. I was driven, and there seemed to be no end in sight.

My intensity hit its pinnacle when I could no longer sleep at night unless I had shared Christ with someone that day. When my head hit the pillow, I'd recall my lack of service. So I'd get up, go to the nearest twenty-four-hour grocery store, and find someone to preach at. Once I said my lines, I could go home and sleep. The response I received wasn't important. "You can't control the outcome," I told myself. I had fulfilled my duty. I had answered the call. And now I could sleep.

> I could no longer sleep at night unless I had shared Christ with someone that day.

Ridiculous? Maybe. But all I was doing was carrying out what I had heard some people suggest to be the path to spiritual growth and fulfillment. My madness seems extreme, but it was nothing more than taking the method presented to me to its ultimate conclusion. I would always have a response ready for those who inquired about my "walk" and wanted to keep me "accountable." They would never label *me* as backslidden or unspiritual. That would hurt worse than carrying out this performance ritual. Or so I thought.

MY END

Soon all the exertion with no payoff took its toll. I began spiraling into a deep depression. A few months later, I found myself lying on the floor of my apartment, sobbing for hours on end: "God, I'm doing everything I'm supposed to do, and I still don't feel closer to you. In fact, I feel worse than ever! How could this have gone so wrong? I can't see any way out. Help me!"

I had no choice but to call home. I picked up the phone, and within hours I had left the university mid-semester to return to my home state of Virginia. I didn't know what awaited me, but I knew I couldn't remain in my current condition.

There was no quick fix. After months of seeking help, I still couldn't break free from my obsession with performing for God. My father got wind of a man who might have answers for me, so we jumped on a plane to Atlanta. After spending a day in prayer with this man, some of my thoughts began to clear up. At least I was able to agree that the compulsions to perform were not coming from God. This was a start.

The following years were not easy. I returned to college, earned my degree, and even went on to graduate school, but I had lost all confidence in who I was. My beliefs had betrayed me. If I were vulnerable enough to be honest during the times I was evangelizing, I would've made the following pitch: "Would you like to become a Christian and be miserable like me?"

So I was in a rebuilding time. I had been broken, stripped of any sense of self-worth. I had gone from class clown and student body president to intense Christian warrior and then to quiet, awkward guy in the corner. Psychologically, I was all over the map. I needed answers.

> "Would you like to become a Christian and be miserable like me?"

MY NEW BEGINNING

It's been seventeen years since I lay sobbing on the floor of that apartment. Today, I wouldn't trade my relationship with God for anything. In fact, I would wish my relationship with him on everyone! Through my desperation, my surrender to God for real answers, and my willingness to leave behind everything I had presumed before, I was introduced to the *naked* gospel.

I was already a Christian, but no one had ever taken the time to strip off all of the convoluted ideas and misleading jargon. No one had ever presented me with the bare truth. What I needed was an intravenous shot that wasn't poisoned with religiosity. Once I realized I was on the wrong path, God enabled me to see his way—the route to freedom.

The content of this book is the result of my journey. Hope began with grasping an important distinction between two operating systems—one Old and one New. Once I saw the doorway to the New, all I had to do was walk through.

What was on the other side was life changing.

2

I'M NOT THE ONLY ONE TO HIT ROCK BOTTOM. APPARENTLY, MANY Christians experience an initial excitement upon accepting Christ but later become disappointed, disillusioned, or even depressed.

Some of America's church leaders have been trying to figure out why this epidemic exists and what can be done about it. In 2004, Willow Creek Community Church in South Barrington, Illinois, developed the REVEAL survey to understand and measure the heart—the emotions and attitudes—of the people who attend Willow Creek. Since then, over four hundred churches of a cross section of sizes, denominations, and regions of the country have used the survey to ask their members questions similar to the ones below.

We'll get into how Christians around the country responded to questions like these. But first, take a moment to decide how you'd answer them. For each question, circle a number between 1 (lowest level) and 10 (highest level) to indicate your answer.

1. How would you rate your level of enthusiasm for church?

    1   2   3   4   5   6   7   8   9   10

2. How would you rate your overall level of fulfillment in life?

    1   2   3   4   5   6   7   8   9   10

3. How would you rate your level of satisfaction with your spiritual growth?

1	2	3	4	5	6	7	8	9	10

4. How would you rate your level of involvement in church-related activities?

1	2	3	4	5	6	7	8	9	10

The Big Surprise

The Willow Creek researchers thought they might find a strong relationship between time spent on church activities and spiritual growth and fulfillment. They presumed that anyone who donated their time to church must be actively growing and fulfilled. That makes sense, right?

As it turns out, wrong.

The survey revealed that it wasn't the more active Christians who were growing and fulfilled. The survey also unveiled a large number—approximately 25 percent of the attendees surveyed at Willow Creek—who admitted they were "stagnant" or "dissatisfied." And other churches are finding this to be true among their attendees as well.

So what's going wrong in churches today? If we spend more time in church, shouldn't we expect to grow spiritually and find fulfillment? Aren't we told that if we drink the living water that Jesus offers, we'll never thirst again? If this is true, then what's happening with so many Christians today? What's missing?

Many of our North American churches seem to have everything—culturally relevant outreach, attractive facilities, and a broad range of programs to match any and every lifestyle. Add to this the experience of dynamic speakers, professional-quality music, and inviting small groups. How could those who are most active in these churches be stagnant and dissatisfied?

There's nothing wrong with top-quality facilities, creative programs, and a genuine sense of community. But the fundamental question is, "What message are we sharing in our community and within our walls through our programs?" I believe it's our *substance*, not our structure, that is leaving so many stagnant and dissatisfied. A church may have polished programs, well-trained staff, and dynamic speakers.

> Many of today's churches seem to have everything.

But *content* is what people walk away with.

THE NAKED GOSPEL QUIZ

To illustrate this point, let's pause for a short quiz. Below are ten faith-related concepts that don't seem to be regularly discussed in many churches today. But our view on each of these concepts affects our relationship with God, our spiritual growth, and our fulfillment in life. So for each of the ten concepts, decide whether you think each is true or false. Simply circle the *T* or *F* next to each statement to indicate your response. (*Note: Don't move on to read the answers until you've responded to each one.*)

1. Christians should ask God to forgive and cleanse them when they sin. T F

2. Christians struggle with sin because of their old self within. T F

3. We should wait on God even before making everyday decisions. T F

4. When we sin against God, we're out of fellowship until we repent. T F

5. Old Testament law is written on Christians' hearts so we want to obey it. T F

6. The Bible tells us that Christians can obtain
   many rewards in heaven.   T   F

7. Christians will give an account for their sins
   at the great white throne.   T   F

8. Christians should tithe at least 10 percent of
   their income to the church.   T   F

9. God gets angry with us when we repeatedly
   sin against him.   T   F

10. God looks at us as though we're righteous,
    even though we're really not.   T   F

QUIZ ANSWERS

Why the quiz? Well, remember the survey you took at the beginning of this chapter? You assessed your *feelings* about church, your *enthusiasm* for life, and your *satisfaction* with your spiritual growth. Inevitably, our thinking leads to feelings. So the only effective way to move toward growth and fulfillment when we're feeling dissatisfied or inexplicably stagnant is to dig deeply into God's Word to find real answers that change our *thinking*.

I lived through the consequences of my thinking, and my recovery came through a decade of slowly learning to replace old thoughts with new ones. I don't know if there is more of a story to tell than my trial and error, suffering under error, and finally getting answers.

Speaking of answers, the biblical answer to each of the naked gospel quiz statements is *false*.

Yes, *false*.

So how'd you do?

Are you ready to peel away layers of religiosity in order to discover an exhilarating reality—always keeping in mind that truth is supposed to set you *free*?

PART 2

religion is a headache

Many Christians still walk in Old Covenant bondage.
Regarding the law as a Divine ordinance for our direction,
they consider themselves prepared and fitted by conversion to
take up the fulfillment of the law as a natural duty.

Andrew Murray (1828 – 1917)

3

MANY NON-CHRISTIANS WHOM I KNOW HAVE PURPOSELY OPTED not to contract the Christian disease. They may call themselves *atheist* or *agnostic*, and they seem to wear the badge proudly. They have, in their minds, wisely avoided the painful symptoms of unnecessary religion.

Maybe it's true that some still say, "Christianity is a crutch." And in essence, those are actually kind words, since a crutch is a support that keeps one from falling. But more recently, the popular line of thinking is "Why would I want to subject myself to something that appears to be making so many miserable?" For many, Christianity is seen more as a cancer than a crutch.

Outsiders are growing wise to the fact that many Christians are dissatisfied with their church or their personal relationship with God. Their faith just isn't working for them anymore as they can't seem to maintain their end of the "bargain" with God. Many Christians may have had an exciting salvation experience and perhaps even a period of fulfilling spiritual growth, but somehow what began as exhilarating and explosive is now fizzling out.

> For many, Christianity is seen more as a cancer than a crutch.

An Ancient Problem

This is *not* a new problem. More than one hundred years ago, Hannah Whitall Smith recounted the following statement made by a friend who was looking in on Christianity from the outside:

> "If you Christians want to make us agnostics inclined to look into your religion, you must try to be more comfortable in the possession of it yourselves. The Christians I meet seem to me to be the very most uncomfortable people anywhere around. They seem to carry their religion as a man carries a headache. He does not want to get rid of his head, but at the same time it is very uncomfortable to have it. And I for one do not care to have that sort of religion."
>
> QUOTED IN HANNAH WHITALL SMITH, *The God of All Comfort*

So if we admit that this problem exists, it is only sensible to seek out a solution. But where do we turn for genuine answers? Perhaps we should begin with understanding the *origin* of the problem better. And, yes, this problem is more than just a hundred years old.

To understand the root of this religious problem, let's journey back thousands of years ago, when the people of Israel gathered to hear what God required of them. Notice that their response was a fully committed *yes*:

> When Moses went and told the people all the LORD's words and laws, they responded with one voice, "Everything the LORD has said we will do." Moses then wrote down everything the LORD had said. . . .
> Then [Moses] took the Book of the Covenant and read it to the people. They responded, "We will do everything the LORD has said; we will obey."
>
> EXODUS 24:3, 7

Over 600 commandments in all—more than 350 items and actions to abstain from and nearly 250 actions on the Jewish to-do list. Oh, and by the way, some violations of the law—such as idolatry and sexual sins—were punishable by death!

So how did the Israelites' commitment play out? Well, you may know the story. The history of Israel as recorded in the Old Testament is one of failure upon failure and disappointment after disappointment.

ROLLER COASTER

God commissioned the tribe of Levi to function as Israel's priests. These priests taught the law, offered animal sacrifices, and prayed for guidance. The high priest officiated in the Most Holy Place on the Day of Atonement. He would enter and sprinkle blood all over the cover of the ark as an offering, first for his own sins and then for the sins of the Israelites. A priest would serve for twenty-five years or until death, at which time the privilege would go to his oldest son. And God mandated that the priesthood remain in the family line of Levi.

Asaph, a Levitical choir director, wrote one of the best encapsulations of Israel's experience under the law. In Psalm 78, we read that God was continually faithful to Israel. He delivered them from slavery in Egypt, dividing the Red Sea and guiding them with a cloud by day and a pillar of fire by night. He split rocks to miraculously provide water and even made food fall from heaven. He proved himself again and again. And all he asked in return was one simple thing—that Israel be faithful.

But Psalm 78 reveals a roller-coaster experience of ups and downs with God—obedience followed by failure, failure followed by a promise to recommit, and then failure once again ensuing. Here's a brief excerpt from Asaph's account:

> But they put God to the test
> > and rebelled against the Most High;
> > they did not keep his statutes.
> Like their ancestors they were disloyal and faithless,
> > as unreliable as a faulty bow.
> They angered him with their high places;
> > they aroused his jealousy with their idols.
> When God heard them, he was furious;
> > he rejected Israel completely.
>
> PSALM 78:56–59

So it appears that the people ended up with egg on their faces. But what about the priests themselves? Perhaps the Levitical line of priests remained faithful to God despite Israel's disobedience?

> "And now, you priests, this warning is for you. If you do not listen, and if you do not resolve to honor my name," says the LORD Almighty, "I will send a curse on you, and I will curse your blessings. Yes, I have already cursed them, because you have not resolved to honor me."
>
> MALACHI 2:1–2

The priests themselves didn't fare much better than the lay-people of Israel. But could it be that the obedience of a nation just takes time to develop? No, even long after the Israelites' exodus from Egypt and well beyond the days of Malachi, we still find the most devout Jewish servant struggling to remain faithful. Saul of Tarsus, perhaps Israel's most committed of all, couldn't seem to fulfill his religious commitments to God: "I do not understand what I do. For *what I want to do I do not do*, but what I hate I do" (Romans 7:15, italics added).

To some, the law appeared to offer a satisfying religious experience and a life of fulfillment. But, one way or another, it pronounced the curse of failure on anyone who attempted to keep it. No one could escape the inevitable outcome. There was certainly nothing wrong with the law itself, but through rule upon rule upon rule, the law clearly showed that there was something wrong with *everyone* in Israel.

FAST-FORWARD

But let's fast-forward a couple of thousand years to the present. It's not just the most committed of Israel who have expressed frustration and misery because of their own religion.

Martin Luther's struggle with his religion is also well documented. Despite Luther's fervor and lifestyle of commitment, he was constantly overcome with guilt. He was infatuated with self-flagellation and made countless attempts to atone for his never-ending list of sins. In addition to whipping himself until he bled, he would sometimes lie down on the snowy ground all night long in the dead of winter until eventually he was in such a state of shock that his colleagues would have to carry him away to safety.

Similarly, in her recently released private writings, Mother Teresa confessed the following: "I am told God loves me—and yet the reality of darkness and coldness and emptiness is so great that nothing touches my soul. Before the work started, there was so much union, love, faith, trust, prayer, and sacrifice. Did I make a mistake in surrendering blindly to the Call of the Sacred Heart?" (addressed to Jesus, at the suggestion of a confessor, undated).

In more than forty years of tireless service, Mother Teresa had an impact on thousands upon thousands of lives. She reached out to the sick, the homeless, and the orphans of her own country and beyond. Still, her private writings reveal a struggle for meaning, purpose, and a stable relationship with God.

> "Did I make a mistake in surrendering blindly to the Call of the Sacred Heart?"

So what do Saul of Tarsus, Martin Luther, and Mother Teresa all have in common? They all appear to have wrestled under a religious system that brought them no enduring sense of satisfaction or accomplishment, but only misery. Their methods of propitiating and thereby approaching their God ultimately led to a deep sense of failure. Having exerted more effort than nearly any of us will ever expend, they probably found themselves saying, "How much is enough? When will it end? Why is God still not satisfied? When do I get to relax and enjoy? There's got to be another way."

ANOTHER WAY

So what if there *is* another way? What if we could do away with *all* of the religious guilt and live from delight? What if we could enjoy so great an intimacy with God that it would seem he was nearly beneath our skin? What if we could just go through life being ourselves and somehow express Christ along the way? And what if all of this could come at no expense of our own? It would mean the religion thing could end. It would mean we wouldn't have to analyze ourselves and measure our spirituality.

There is an Old way that forever leads to disappointment, no matter how much "holy" effort is exerted. There is also a New way that comes free of charge and changes everything. And yet there is also a third option—a hybrid of Old and New that you find in many churches today.

This book is intended to reveal the futility of the Old and the ecstasy of the New. Most important, we'll talk about how to escape the misery of today's hybrid religiosity and enjoy the purity of the New. The New is what God intended all along for the dedicated but miserable people throughout history.

And the New is what God intends for you.

4

Put yourself in the place of your favorite Old Testament character for a moment. Imagine what it would be like to be them. Perhaps you'd like to be David or Esther or Daniel.

What closeness they had with God! How they walked with him and were used by him! Wouldn't it be great to be one of them? Perhaps you'd be willing to trade your own relationship with God for theirs instead? If so, I couldn't agree with you less.

Less?

That's right, less.

Not in a million years would I want David's relationship with God over my own. Nor Esther's. Nor Daniel's. Nor any Old Testament figure's. I much prefer what I have right now.

How arrogant!

How bold!

I hope I've startled you and perhaps even ruffled your feathers a bit, because I intend to. I believe it's time for the church to wake up and realize how good we have it today on this side of the cross.

You may know about the famous heroes of the faith mentioned in Hebrews 11 — people such as Abraham, Isaac, Jacob, Joseph, and Moses. Through the author of Hebrews, God tells of their commitment, their sacrifice, and their surrender to his ways.

These heroes were mocked, imprisoned, and even stoned to death because of their faith.

Have you been tested to such lengths? Have you proven to be equally committed? Likely, the answer is *no.* Then how could you possibly obtain a better relationship with God than they had?

Before we answer the *how,* let's make sure that this is indeed the case. Referring to Old Testament believers, the author of Hebrews writes, "These were all commended for their faith, yet *none of them received* what had been promised. God had planned *something better for us* so that only together with us would they be made perfect" (Hebrews 11:39–40, italics added).

Such dedication, such commitment—yet what do we learn about these heroes of Old? They did *not* receive what was promised. And on this side of the cross, we possess something better than they ever enjoyed.

> God is the same as he has always been.

What is it that makes our situation better than theirs? Has God changed? Certainly not. God is the same as he has always been. Then what is it exactly that makes today so different from 2,000 or so years ago?

It has everything to do with the New.

PAPERS, PLEASE!

Imagine being a fly on the wall during a hypothetical dialogue between Moses and Jesus of Nazareth. "Papers, please," Moses exclaims. But Jesus of Nazareth would have no papers, at least none that would meet the requirements. The law required that a person be from the tribe of Levi to qualify as high priest, but Jesus was from the tribe of Judah. No one from Judah's line had ever served as priest. The law forbade such a selection.

Today, Christians regard Jesus Christ as their high priest, but according to the law, Jesus as high priest makes no sense at all.

How then can we rightfully look to Jesus as our priest today? If the priestly line has changed, then the whole system for relating to God has to be replaced. And that's exactly what has happened—the *whole* system has changed!

It's crucial to realize that the law and Jesus just don't mix. "[Jesus] ... belonged to a different tribe, and no one from that tribe has ever served at the altar. For it is clear that our Lord descended from Judah, and in regard to that tribe Moses said nothing about priests" (Hebrews 7:13–14). Christians talk about Jesus as their Savior, their Lord, and the author (priest) of their forgiveness. Some of these same believers then claim that the law is still for us today. In so doing, they adhere to a major contradiction.

The issue of law and grace (Old and New) is certainly still hotly debated today: Do we live by law? Do we live by grace? Do we live by a combination of the two? Doesn't God write the law on our hearts? Despite the countless pages in Christian books devoted to these questions, Jesus' lineage fails to take center stage. We can propose all kinds of theories, compromises, and answers concerning law and grace, but one fact remains: the law discredits Jesus as priest. For this reason, the writer of Hebrews writes, "When the priesthood is changed, the law must be changed also" (Hebrews 7:12).

The bottom line is that if you appeal to Jesus as your priest, what place is there for the law in your life? You call on a man from Nazareth, from the tribe of Judah, who shares no family lineage with Aaron, or Levi, or any other qualified priest of the law. You call on an outsider, a renegade, a table turner.

GOD'S NEW DEAL

Christians readily accept the idea that Jesus is their priest. But it's not clear to some that, through their adoption of Jesus as priest, they enter into a contract with God, an agreement, a covenant. In contrast to the old contract that God penned through Moses, this new one will never be replaced. It's the final word concerning a human's relationship with God. Jesus Christ is the author and guarantee of something totally new and revolutionary:

> For this reason Christ is the mediator of a new covenant, that those who are called may receive the promised eternal inheritance.
>
> HEBREWS 9:15

> "The Lord has sworn
>   and will not change his mind:
>   'You are a priest forever.'"

> Because of this oath, Jesus has become the guarantor of a better covenant.
>
> HEBREWS 7:21–22

A new covenant? What does that mean? I attended churches for more than a decade before hearing even a single teaching about the new covenant. But if we want to understand how God relates to us, we should look to the New. The New and the Old are certainly not the same.

Here's a quote from God himself on the matter:

> The days are coming, declares the Lord,
>   when I will make a new covenant
> with the house of Israel
>   and with the house of Judah.
> *It will not be like the covenant*
>   I made with their ancestors
> when I took them by the hand
>   to lead them out of Egypt,
> because they did not remain faithful to my covenant,
>   and I turned away from them,
>   declares the Lord.
>
> HEBREWS 8:8–9, italics added

Something new was coming all along. God always intended to usher in something radically different. This passage indicates that the New is unlike anything before, and that it solves a serious problem—our failure to remain faithful. Whatever the New is, it somehow *causes* people to remain faithful, even when their own strength fails them.

Today we debate eternal security, but security (or faithfulness) was an Old issue. Apparently, one reason the New came on the scene was to cure that problem: "For if there had been nothing wrong with that first covenant, no place would have been sought for another. But God found fault with the people" (Hebrews 8:7–8).

There was really nothing wrong with the Old in itself. It should still be esteemed as holy and good. The issue with the Old was that no one could operate successfully under it. For that reason, God orchestrated a different way.

The New involves God's desires being written inside us, so that we have the guarantee of being his people no matter what:

> No one could operate successfully under the Old.

> "This is the covenant I will establish
>   with the house of Israel
>   after that time, declares the Lord.
> I will put my laws in their minds
>   and write them on their hearts.
> I will be their God,
>   and they will be my people."
>
> HEBREWS 8:10

We glean some important insights from God's own description of the New. God inscribes his laws on our minds and hearts. We become his people and have the privilege of knowing him personally. But the author of Hebrews actually *misquotes* the Old Testament passage here. How could he be so bold? And for what reason? He purposely changes the Old Testament rendition "my law" to "my laws" to clarify an important truth: Contrary to popular teaching, it's not the law of Moses that is written on our hearts.

It's God's laws.

These are expounded on by Jesus and the New Testament writers. These laws are called "the royal law" (James 2:8), "the law that gives freedom" (James 1:25; 2:12), and "[Jesus'] commands" (1 John 3:24). God's commandments are to love him and to love each other (Mark 12:30–31). These aren't burdensome. In fact, Jesus himself says that those who love him *will* obey his commands (John 14:15). Under the New, God has it rigged.

> It's not the law of Moses that is written on our hearts.

If the Mosaic law were written on our hearts and minds, imagine the consequences! The dietary restrictions, the wardrobe regulations, and hundreds of other rules would overwhelm our consciences, just as they did the Israelites'.

Thank God that the New isn't just a dressed-up version of the Old!

The New is different, and simple.

5

IN 1998, MY FATHER WAS KILLED IN A CAR ACCIDENT. MY FATHER was a loving husband, a successful businessman, and a great dad. His intellect was only rivaled by his sense of humor. He is greatly missed in our family.

Imagine for a moment that you and I sit down to dinner, and I take the opportunity to break out the family album to show you photos of my dad. As I turn pages, point to photos, and tell stories about him, something unpredictable happens. By some miracle, my father suddenly walks through the door! Strangely, though, I keep pointing at photos and telling old stories. Even after I notice his arrival, I still seem to be occupied with the album.

Ridiculous, right? Why would I fixate on a two-dimensional photo of my father when the real thing is standing right in front of me?

But in the same way, some Christians are fixated on the law when it's only a shadow. The reality, we're told, is found in the New.

> Some Christians are fixated on the law when it's only a shadow.

To look to the Old after learning of the New is like my returning to my dad's photo album when he's standing right there. I am caught up in something two-dimensional and lifeless, even as his living presence is with me.

Here is God's announcement about the superiority of the New: "The ministry Jesus has received is as superior to theirs as the covenant of which he is mediator is superior to the old one, since the new covenant is established on better promises" (Hebrews 8:6).

If the law were able to save, there'd be no reason for the New. The Old is old news. Something greater is now in effect, so why wouldn't we hold fast to the New?

Interestingly, even Old Testament believers were justified by faith alone, apart from the law. Does the law involve faith? No, the Bible clearly shows that "the Law is not of faith" (Galatians 3:12 NASB). After all, does it take faith to adhere to regulations and carry out religious tasks?

> "The Law is not of faith" (Galatians 3:12).

Old Testament saints such as Abraham were made right because they put confidence in God and in a coming Messiah (Romans 4:13). Abraham lived *long before* the law, but he was declared righteous. So being right with God never had anything to do with the law.

CAR TROUBLE

Imagine that you put aside money to purchase a brand-new car. Once you have enough saved, you call the dealership to negotiate a price. Fortunately, the dealer agrees to let the car go at a price you can afford. Within the hour, you're in the dealership to close the deal. The price with delivery charges, taxes, and tags comes out to $19,550.00. A great deal. You happily sign the paperwork and take the car home. It's finally yours!

More than a year later, you receive a peculiar message in your voice mailbox. It's from the dealership. You recognize the salesman's voice as he explains that he accidentally charged you *too little* for the vehicle. He says you owe $2,000.00 more on the car. He invites you to the dealership so you can redraft the sales contract and "work things out."

After the message ends, you stand there in disbelief. You look at the calendar and begin counting the days. It's been 430 days since you signed the contract to purchase the car! How can they do this? *Can* they do this? It's time to call your attorney.

Your legal counsel explains that the dealership is out of line. They can't require you to change the terms of the contract you signed 430 days ago. If they could force a person to renegotiate after signing, no one would ever place confidence in a contract.

Now see if you can catch the parallel between your car purchase turned sour and Paul's point about the New — the New that was promised to Abraham:

> Even though it is only a man's covenant, yet when it has been ratified, no one sets it aside or adds conditions to it.... What I am saying is this: the Law, which came four hundred and thirty years later, *does not invalidate a covenant previously ratified* by God, so as to nullify the promise.
>
> GALATIANS 3:15, 17 NASB, italics added

The promise of the New was made to Abraham not 430 days but 430 years *before* the law. Just as the car dealership couldn't legally renegotiate a contract previously signed, the covenant made to Abraham was not renegotiated just because the law came on the scene later.

Although not in effect yet, the New was promised to Abraham and ratified by God himself. The fact that 430 years later the law was introduced does not affect the stipulations of the covenant previously ratified. So hundreds of years separate the promise of the New from the Old. We shouldn't mix

> Hundreds of years separate the promise of the New from the Old.

them together, nor should we extract elements from the Old and impose them on the New. That's a breach of contract.

While introducing the New, we've already spent significant time in Hebrews. Hebrews may well be the least-studied epistle among Christians today. Essentially, it's a lengthy argument for abandonment of the Old and adoption of the New. Its style reads like that of a brilliant trial lawyer, and Hebrews alone can put to rest many of the issues dividing Christians today. Throughout *The Naked Gospel*, you'll get to know Hebrews and other New Testament letters that shout in unison, "Jesus plus nothing."

6

HAVE YOU EVER HAD TO SLIP ON SOMEONE ELSE'S SHOES? IF SO, YOU know what it's like to wear something that's not made for you. At first glance, the shoes may appear similar to any of your own. But they simply don't match the dimensions of your foot.

In the same way, we're informed that the law of Moses is indeed for someone — but it's *not* a good fit for New Testament believers. Paul wrote to Timothy:

> We know that the law is good if one uses it properly. We also know that *the law is made not for the righteous* but for lawbreakers and rebels, the ungodly and sinful, the unholy and irreligious .... And it is for whatever else is contrary to the sound doctrine that conforms to the gospel concerning the glory of the blessed God, which he entrusted to me.
>
> 1 TIMOTHY 1:8–11, italics added

What purpose does the law serve? Paul says that it is exclusively for *un*believers. Under the Old, God recognized two kinds of people — Jews and Gentiles. Today, he recognizes two different groups — believers and unbelievers. In the Old Testament, the law was only for Jews. Today, the law speaks to only one group, namely, unbelievers.

So if you're a Christian, what place should the law have in your life?

SHUT UP!

The law has one intended audience—unbelievers. But what is the law saying to them? And what is the typical response when the law speaks? The best way to summarize the law's message is by using an expression that was forbidden in my home as I was growing up: "Shut up!" My mother never tolerated that phrase. But this is precisely what the law says to the unbeliever. In fact, the whole world is silenced by the law:

> The law has one intended audience — unbelievers.

> Now we know that whatever the law says, it says to those who are under the law, so that every mouth may be silenced and the whole world held accountable to God. Therefore no one will be declared righteous in his sight by observing the law; rather, through the law we become conscious of sin.
>
> ROMANS 3:19–20

Sometimes people aren't listening. If you want their attention, you have to shout. Through the law, God shouts that he demands no less than perfection. When we see the standard, we have no choice but to "shut up." Our mouths are silenced. We're not empowered to try harder. Nor are we safe just giving up and making a go at it without righteousness. We're caught in a predicament. And without intervention, we'd remain in a bewildered state.

Like Adam and Eve, we become conscious of our nakedness before God. But there's no covering on earth that will hide our unrighteousness. The law exposes our addiction to sin and our need for Christ:

> Why the Law then?... But the Scripture has shut up everyone under sin, so that the promise by faith in Jesus Christ might be given to those who believe.
>
> GALATIANS 3:19, 22 NASB

Once in a while, I have the privilege of speaking to prison inmates about the gospel. Some of the men are under life sentences. They'll be locked up until they die. As I enter these prisons, and the heavy metal doors close behind me, I imagine what it'd be like to be incarcerated. (I've even imagined a mistake with the paperwork that leaves me trapped inside!)

Being held prisoner, locked up indefinitely, is not generally seen as desirable. But this is precisely how Paul describes life under the law. It's like being locked up as a prisoner:

> Before this faith came, we were held prisoners by the law, locked up until faith should be revealed. So the law was put in charge to lead us to Christ that we might be justified by faith.
>
> GALATIANS 3:23–24 NIV

Being under the law is like being in prison. You're constantly reminded that you're guilty and awaiting your sentence. The law doesn't encourage us, nor does it build us up. With its perfect standard, it only tears down our pride. It shows us that we'll never succeed. As Paul says, the law has been "put in charge to lead us to Christ." How does it lead us to Christ? By showing us our spiritual death and our need for new life.

> Being under the law is like being in prison.

DRIVERS EXCELLENCE AWARD

As a teenager, I accrued many violations in my pursuit of speed on America's highways. I seldom struggled with the most common temptations that teens deal with. But for some reason, the allure of a speeding automobile always seemed to get the better of me.

For a few years, I was constantly receiving warnings and speeding tickets. I was even once charged with reckless driving due to excessive speed. Of course, there were times when I would feel remorse for my actions—and I'd slow down for a while. But nothing really curbed my addiction to speed.

But imagine, as I make my way to school one morning, driving at the legal speed limit, I notice the familiar flashing blue lights in my rearview mirror. So I pull over to the side of the road and watch as the police officer exits his patrol car and motions for me to roll down my window.

But strangely, the officer has a friendly smile on his face this time. Let's say he approaches my window with a gleam in his eye and says, "Mr. Farley, I just wanted to say thank you for driving at a safe speed. You're a good man. The state of Virginia appreciates your efforts to keep our highways safe. This morning, I want to award you the Virginia Drivers Excellence Award. This award includes a certificate redeemable for merchandise at any Division of Motor Vehicles office. Congratulations." Then he hands me the certificate and says, "You have a great day!"

Wow! I would be stunned, wouldn't you? Of course you would, because episodes like this don't find their way into our lives very often. In fact, I doubt if anything like this has ever happened. I've never heard of a police officer pulling someone over in order to compliment them on their good driving.

Legalism will never produce love.

For some reason, the law only gives us its attention when we are in the wrong.

Similarly, the law of Moses only points out where we've fallen short. Looking for love and encouragement? You'll never find them in the law. This is why the strictest legalist you know can fabricate an appearance of morality. But legalism will never produce love. Living under a law mentality is like being a slave to a most demanding taskmaster. There's always more to do. And you'll *never* do enough to please him. James teaches, "Whoever keeps the whole law and yet stumbles at just one point is guilty of breaking *all* of it" (James 2:10, italics added).

PASS OR FAIL

Keeping 1 percent or 99 percent of the law is one and the same. Imagine a person who's able to abide by most of the law. Let's say they only struggle occasionally with one tiny regulation. But whether we obey none of the law or most of the law, we're still cursed under it. As the apostle Paul states, "All who rely on observing the law are *under a curse*, for it is written: 'Cursed is everyone who does not continue to do *everything* written in the Book of the Law'" (Galatians 3:10, italics added).

How can Paul be so extreme in his view? We know that Paul (formerly Saul) was a man who tried to obey every aspect of the law. Speaking of himself to the Philippians, he even writes, "... as for righteousness based on the law, [I was found] faultless" (Philippians 3:6).

Those around Paul may have thought he was blameless. But Paul knew better. He was acquainted with the failure that all of us find when we try to obey the law. Speaking of his failure, Paul writes:

> I would not have known what sin was had it not been for the law. For I would not have known what coveting really was if the law had not said, "You shall not covet." But sin, seizing the opportunity afforded by the commandment, produced in me every kind of coveting.
>
> ROMANS 7:7–8

Law is an all-or-nothing proposition. Either you comply with every ounce of the law, or you're cursed. There's no other option. Do we have a right to pick and choose from the law? Or have we been awarded the luxury of mixing a portion of the law with Christ? Paul warns that if we add even a pinch of law to our life in Christ, he'll be of no value to us:

> Law is an all-or-nothing proposition.

> Mark my words! I, Paul, tell you that if you let your-selves be circumcised, Christ will be of no value to you at all. Again I declare to every man who lets himself be circumcised that *he is obligated to obey the whole law.*
>
> GALATIANS 5:2–3, italics added

It's preposterous for Christians to adopt portions of the law of Moses as our guide for living. We're presuming that God grades on a curve. But the law is completely incompatible with our attempt to "do our best." Law is a pass-or-fail system.

And one strike means you're out.

7

In the United States, some Christians fight for the Ten Commandments to be posted on our public buildings. We say that we don't want our society to lose its Christian roots.

But Christianity was never rooted in the law, not even in the Ten Commandments.

Law Breeds Sin

The commandments aren't intended to supervise Christians. They don't curb sinful desires. In fact, the law causes *more* sinning:

> While we were in the flesh, *the sinful passions, which were aroused by the Law,* were at work in the members of our body to bear fruit for death.
>
> Romans 7:5 NASB, italics added

> But sin, seizing *the opportunity afforded by the commandment,* produced in me every kind of coveting. For apart from the law, sin was dead.
>
> Romans 7:8, italics added

Will living by the Ten Commandments result in a godly life? Paul leads us to the opposite conclusion. Theologians debate about whether Paul is speaking of his saved or his lost condition in Romans 7, but regardless, the main point is that, saved or lost, human beings *cannot keep the law.* The law continually excites sin.

The law arouses sinful passions. Sin gains opportunity through the law. This is what Romans 7 explains. So does a Christian life that involves trying to perfectly live by the Ten Commandments sound promising? Paul discovered what every human realizes when they truly give law their best shot: the law kills. Just as God intended, Moses introduced a ministry of *condemnation.*

> The law continually excites sin.

Recently, a popular humor book documented the journey of a man who attempted to live by the regulations in the Old Testament for one solid year.* He detailed for us what this kind of life would look like in modern-day America. He altered his diet to exclude certain meats and seafood. He excluded from his wardrobe anything spun of more than one kind of material. And he even engaged in animal sacrifices of sorts! In the end, he candidly and humorously concluded that he could not adhere to even a majority of the regulations in the Old Testament. He also documents the convoluted reasoning of some of his fellow Jewish people, who have decided that things are somehow different today and that they don't have to adhere to *all* of the law's restrictions —just to some of them.

THE TEN

Many agree that the ceremonial law, restricting everything from diet to wardrobe, is not for Christians today. Indeed, few Christians attempt to follow those regulations. But should Christians still look to the Ten Commandments as their moral guide?

When Paul talks about the law arousing sinful passions, he

---

*A. J. Jacobs, *The Year of Living Biblically* (New York: Simon and Schuster, 2007).

uses coveting as his example. Paul reveals that one of the Ten Commandments excited sin in his life. Sin used "You shall not covet" to compel Paul to exert human effort to stop coveting. And the natural result occurred—coveting. When fleshly effort tries to overcome sin, sin wins every time. So Paul ended up struggling with coveting *of every kind.*

I find it amusing that a fervent religious leader couldn't stop craving other people's stuff! Sure, Saul of Tarsus could polish his exterior. But inside he was guilty of wanting others' possessions.

Paul's mantra might as well have been, "I fought the law, and the law won."

In 2 Corinthians, we see evidence that the Ten Commandments bring nothing but condemnation and death:

> Now if the ministry that brought death, which was *engraved in letters on stone,* came with glory, so that the Israelites could not look steadily at the face of Moses because of its glory, transitory though it was, will not the ministry of the Spirit be even more glorious? If the ministry that brought condemnation was glorious, how much more glorious is the ministry that brings righteousness!
>
> 2 CORINTHIANS 3:7–9, italics added

How do we know that Paul is referring to the Ten Commandments and not to some ceremonial regulations? He specifically mentions that this ministry "was engraved in letters on stone." This was true only of the commandments. So it was a ministry designed to condemn.

If we live under the law, sin will dominate us. If we live free from law (under grace), sin won't overpower us: "Sin shall no longer be your master, because you are not under the law, but under grace" (Romans 6:14).

The freedom from sin's power that we all desire is right under our noses. The obstacle to experiencing victory over temptation is *the way in which we've gone about the battle*. When we arm ourselves with the law, we set ourselves up for failure every time.

We may call it *self-discipline* or *accountability*—or plug in some other inventive term. But when it's anything but dependency on Christ within us, it'll inevitably put the wheels of human effort in motion. Perspective is everything in our battle against sin.

But, you may ask, doesn't God help us keep the law?

> When we arm ourselves with the law, we set ourselves up for failure.

If we take this to its ultimate conclusion, then wouldn't the Holy Spirit motivate us to avoid pork, wear clothing woven with only linen, isolate friends and family members who have skin diseases, and refrain from working Friday night through Saturday night? This would mean canceling barbecues, throwing out nylon stockings, terminating Friday night emails, and skipping Saturday yard work. Is this the intention of the Spirit of God in your life?

Think about it.

CHIHUAHUA

"Hold on just a minute!" one of them shouted at me. "You're taking things to an extreme. I agree that the Holy Spirit doesn't want to help us live under the whole book of Leviticus, but we should still follow the Ten Commandments. And we should ask for the Spirit's help to do so!"

I was in the midst of conducting a two-day seminar for pastors, seminary students, and church leaders in Chihuahua, Mexico. It was day two, and our attendance had grown from forty on the first day to about two hundred on the second day. Excitement was growing, and it seemed that people were being set free from the oppression of religiosity.

We were taking a break, and I was sipping my coffee. The next thing I knew, I was surrounded by four leaders who were angrier than hornets. After several minutes of absorbing heated comments, I realized that what angered them the most was my insistence that Christians are even free from the Ten Commandments.

"But Sabbath observance is *included* in the Ten Commandments, and you don't adhere to the Friday night till Saturday night Jewish Sabbath, do you?" I asked.

"Well, no."

"So then, it's the Big Nine that you're under, excluding the Sabbath?"

At that point, the break ended, and we ended our discussion. "Just something to consider," I remarked as we went back to the seminar room.

Poor Substitute

God never gave us permission to divide the law into our favorite pieces so that we could select how much we're under. He delivered us from the entirety of the law by fulfilling it through Jesus Christ. Now we don't have to fulfill *any* of the law.

But how do we live upright lives if we don't use the Ten Commandments as our guide? After hearing that believers have no need for the law, this is a natural question. The short answer is this: The Holy Spirit comes to live inside of us when we believe, and *he is enough*! The fruit that comes from the Holy Spirit within us is enough. And "against such things there is no law" (Galatians 5:23).

The New Testament teaches that those who are *led by the Spirit* are not under the law. The law is a poor substitute for the counsel of the Holy Spirit. We may think that placing ourselves under the

Ten Commandments is a good way to clean house. But law-directed living has the opposite effect. The only sensible choice is *to allow Christ to be himself through us.* This is God's way of impacting our lives and placing his life on display.

> The law is a poor substitute for the counsel of the Holy Spirit.

Some say, "I don't live under the law of Moses. I know I'm free from those commandments. Instead, I live by 'Christian principles.'" This is a fine-sounding variation on what is still a law-based approach. And it's an obstacle to enjoying the dependency-based life. We know that living a "good life" by moral standards is an obstacle to understanding salvation. But choosing "morality" can even prevent a Christian from depending solely on Christ. For Christians, a hidden hindrance to the grace life is a "great" life.

THE ALLURE OF RULES

Principles, rules, and standards—no matter how "Christian" we believe they are—are poor substitutes for a life animated by God himself. In Colossians, we read about rules and their lack of value for Christians:

> Since you died with Christ to the elemental spiritual forces of this world, why, as though you still belonged to the world, do you submit to its rules: "Do not handle! Do not taste! Do not touch!"? These rules, which have to do with things that are all destined to perish with use, are based on merely human commands and teachings. Such regulations indeed have *an appearance of wisdom,* with their self-imposed worship, their false humility and their harsh treatment of the body, but they *lack any value in restraining sensual indulgence.*
>
> COLOSSIANS 2:20–23, italics added

Paul recognizes the allure of principles, commands, and regulations as the means to self-improvement. But he dismisses these as powerless to bring about any real change in our lives. Notice that he's not talking about the means to salvation here. He's referring to our approach to life *after* we've died with Christ.

How will true worship take place? What brings about real humility? What brings actual victory over sin in our lives? Paul is addressing the *daily life* of a believer. And he emphatically states that rules and regulations are not the way to go.

Some might say, "I know that living by rules doesn't save me. But now that I'm saved, I need rules to guide me." That is exactly what the Galatians were saying, compelling Paul to write the following:

> I would like to learn just one thing from you: Did you receive the Spirit by observing the law, or by believing what you heard? Are you so foolish? After beginning with the Spirit, are you now trying to finish by human effort?
>
> GALATIANS 3:2–3

Paul is speaking here to Christians who have already received the Spirit but are returning to the law as a means of self-improvement. They received the Spirit through faith, and he exhorts them not to finish with human effort!

This and similar passages throughout the New Testament address the issue of *daily living*. Paul dispels the myth that God is pleased with rule-based approaches to "perfecting" ourselves. Paul would ask us the same thing today: "Isn't the presence of the resurrected Christ inside of you enough?"

8

GOD DOESN'T WANT BELIEVERS TO BE MOTIVATED BY THE LAW OR BY rules. But it's important to clarify what I'm *not* saying here.

The law itself isn't sinful. Law-haters, known as antinomians, have been misinterpreting the Scriptures since the days of the early church. They say that the law is evil. In combating this false doctrine, the apostle Paul notes that the law isn't sin. In fact, he declares it to be holy, righteous, and good: "So then, the law is holy, and the commandment is holy, righteous and good" (Romans 7:12).

So there's nothing imperfect about the law itself. It's without blemish. The accurate position on the law is *not* that it's flawed. But its perfect standard when combined with human effort results in failure. In short, the law is perfect, but it makes no one perfect.

HERE TO STAY

The law hasn't disappeared just because we have the New. It is still at work today as a tool to convict the unbelieving world. As the words of Jesus indicate, the law will continue to be an ever-present force until heaven and earth disappear:

> Do not think that I have come to abolish the Law or the
> Prophets; I have not come to abolish them but to fulfill

them. Truly I tell you, until heaven and earth disappear, not the smallest letter, not the least stroke of a pen, will by any means disappear from the Law until everything is accomplished.

MATTHEW 5:17–18

Jesus' statement may appear to contradict Paul in Ephesians. Paul talks about the barrier wall between Jew and Gentile (the law) being abolished:

For he himself is our peace, who has made the two one and has destroyed the barrier, the dividing wall of hostility, by setting aside in his flesh the law with its commands and regulations.

EPHESIANS 2:14–15

Paul's words are sometimes misinterpreted to mean that the law has been obliterated. But this would contradict Jesus' teaching that the law will endure as long as this world. Paul's meaning, it seems, is that the law is irrelevant to life in Christ. Both Jew and Gentile are now saved by the same grace. The distinguishing element that separated Jew from Gentile is no more. This is very different from saying that the law has been obliterated.

Maybe the clearest statement concerning the law's usefulness today was written to Timothy: "We know that

> The law is irrelevant to life in Christ.

the law is good if one uses it properly. We also know that law is made not for the righteous ..." (1 Timothy 1:8–9a). Here we see a balanced view of the law. The law still exists and has a purpose today. But it's not designed for Christians as a tool or guide for daily living. Its sole purpose is to convict the ungodly of their spiritually dead state.

Understanding the law's place in the world today keeps us from the error of antinomianism ("law hating"). Understanding that the law has no place in the life of a Christian keeps us from the error of legalism.

FULFILLED

So God's purpose is *not* to fulfill the law within Christians today. Why not? Because he has already fulfilled it.* Hence, the Holy Spirit is not trying to bring Christians into subjection to the law. Nor is he helping Christians comply with it. Jesus already met the requirements of the law. And those who are born of the Spirit have the law's requirements credited to them:

> What the law was powerless to do in that it was weakened by the flesh, *God did* by sending his own Son in the likeness of sinful humanity to be a sin offering. And so he condemned sin in human flesh, *in order that the righteous requirement of the law might be fully met in us,* who do not live according to the flesh but according to the Spirit.
>
> ROMANS 8:3–4, italics added

God did something *in the past* and *fully met* the law's requirements. He sent his Son to be a sin offering, so he could condemn sin. Did God succeed? Of course. When did he succeed? Nearly two thousand years ago. So is God still trying to fulfill the law today? No, he has fulfilled it already. It's a past event.

> Our righteousness is greater than all of the Pharisees' efforts combined.

Notice that God did this so that the law would be fully met *in* us, not *by* us. When we come to Christ, all that he did to fulfill the law is placed *in* us and credited to us. This makes our righteousness greater than all of the Pharisees' efforts combined, even from the first day we believe.

*See Sidelight 1 on p. 229.

"DEAD TO ME"

In Mafia movies, you'll sometimes see a disappointed don inform his son that their relationship is over. The don exclaims, "Son, you're dead to me." The son fixes his gaze on the floor, and tears stream down his cheeks. He slowly leaves the room and his family forever. The connection between him and his father is over. The son is severed from the family, never to be reconnected.

Romans tells us we're *dead to the law*. Just as the Mafia don was disappointed with his son's performance, "Don Law" is disappointed with us. We're not able to perform well enough to stay on his good side. Living under his roof was killing us.

So what was God's solution? God made us die to the law so that we could be reborn into a new family and enjoy a newfound freedom. As Paul writes, "Through the law I died to the law so that I might live for God" (Galatians 2:19).

The moment we die to the Law family, we're picked up by a family of far greater influence. Since we're part of a new family, we're no longer under the demands of "Don Law":

> So, my brothers and sisters, you also *died to the law* through the body of Christ, that you might belong to another, to him who was raised from the dead .... But now, by *dying to what once bound us*, we have been released from the law so that we serve in the new way of the Spirit, and not in the old way of the written code.
>
> ROMANS 7:4, 6, italics added

Remember that the law came in so that sin might *increase*, not decrease (Romans 5:20). God knew the effects of the law. Through the law, we become conscious of sin. Through the law, we die. The law kills. When we realize this, we're ready for a new approach altogether.

COLOMBIAN CADAVER

As a child, my wife, Katharine, lived in Colombia, South America, with her parents who served there as missionaries for four years. In Colombia, Katharine visited some of the most legalistic churches imaginable. Elders and deacons who were well respected among their peers were caught with other men's wives. Admired church leaders turned out to be drunks, compulsive gamblers, or extortionists.

Perhaps the most amazing event was when a man's car blew up in his own driveway, apparently an assassination. The charred body was recovered from the flames, and a funeral was held for the man. About a year later, the man was found alive and well in another city—married to another woman! It turns out he had dug up a cadaver from the cemetery and staged his own death. Apparently, he carried out this charade because of the extensive gambling debts he owed to the local mafia.

Katharine witnessed both extreme legalism and extreme immorality at the same time. Those outrageous events served to illustrate an important point about life under the law. We can dress up, play church, and gain the respect of those around us through the trumpeting of our strict religious rules. But no amount of window dressing can change reality. Sooner or later, life under law will evidence itself.

In Christ, we die and are reborn—free from the law. So we don't have to pretend. Playing church leads to *more* sinning every time.

9

SO WE'RE FREE FROM THE LAW, BUT WHAT ABOUT THINGS SUCH AS Sabbath observance and tithing? We can't leave these issues unaddressed, as they will rob believers of their freedom just as any other part of the law does.

Yes, weekly Sabbath observance and tithing are rooted in the law. If we impose these on believers today, we must likewise observe the remainder of the law. The law is an all-or-nothing system. Adopting portions of it is not an option.

TODAY'S SABBATH

For the Jews, the Sabbath was essentially a reminder of the seventh day of creation, in which God rested after his work. Accordingly, God mandated that Israel *remember* the Sabbath day and reserve it for rest.

Today, we too look back on the finished work of creation. We exclaim along with King David how creative and beautiful the universe is (Psalms 8; 19). But a greater feat than creation has been accomplished—the redemptive work of Jesus Christ on the cross. Just as God declared his creation "good" and then rested, Jesus announced from Calvary, "It is finished!" and then sat down at God's right hand.

The author of Hebrews invites us to rest along with God. We rest by ceasing from the dead works we thought would gain us favor with God. Rather than performing religious acrobatics to rid ourselves of sins, we can sit down with Jesus. We can simply agree, "Yes, it's finished." This is entering God's rest. This is celebrating today's Sabbath:

> There remains, then, *a Sabbath-rest for the people of God*; for those who enter God's rest also *rest from their own work*, as God did from his. Let us, therefore, make every effort to enter that rest.
>
> HEBREWS 4:9–11, italics added

It is possible to calculate the height of a tree by measuring its shadow on the ground. If you look at the shadow, it also gives you a sense of the basic shape of the tree. In a shadow, you have a means to make estimations about the reality. In the Sabbath, the Jews had only a shadow of the reality. The reality is Christ, and a genuine Sabbath-rest is found in him. It's mind-boggling to think about the thousands of years that Jews honored the shadow, the Sabbath. And on this side of the cross we can experience the reality of rest in Christ!

> The reality is Christ, and a genuine Sabbath-rest is found in him.

ROBBING GOD?

Many who realize their freedom from a weekly Sabbath observance still claim that God requires no less than 10 percent of your income. If you don't give at least that much to the church, they say you're "robbing God." But where does the idea of tithing come from?

Joseph's brother Levi was the forefather of a unique tribe called the Levites. When the Israelites escaped from Egypt and conquered the land God promised, they divided the new territory by tribe. But the Levites didn't receive land to cultivate and grow food. Instead, they were instructed to serve as priests in the tabernacle.

Under the law, priests weren't permitted to own homes, property, or possessions. So how did this tribe of priests survive? By means of the support received from the other tribes. So tithing, or giving 10 percent, to these priests was mandated by the law. In this way, God's tribe of priests could maintain an acceptable standard of living while serving him full-time.

Christian teaching today about giving is often inconsistent. If a pastor or church leader uses the term *tithing* and mandates 10 percent as the standard for giving, he is teaching law. If we were to examine this same leader's life, we might see a glaring inconsistency. He owns a home, property, and possessions! He may also be earning additional income from presiding at weddings, writing books, or serving as a seminary professor. The same law that mandates a 10 percent tithe doesn't allow him to do what he's doing.

> If a pastor uses the term *tithing* and mandates 10 percent as the standard for giving, he is teaching law.

Besides one historical reference to Abraham's respect for a foreign priest, Melchizedek, and paying him a tithe from his spoils of war (Hebrews 7:6), there's no other mention of the term *tithe* in the biblical epistles. So what should giving look like under the New? God wants believers to give

- according to the need (2 Corinthians 8:14)
- according to what they have (2 Corinthians 8:11–12)
- not out of guilt or compulsion (2 Corinthians 9:7)
- cheerfully from the heart (2 Corinthians 9:7)

I believe that we church leaders should present liberation from the 10 percent tithe alongside the teaching of freewill giving. Believers are free to give 1 percent, 10 percent, or 100 percent. Clarity concerning grace giving is necessary for a healthy church.

For us to teach anything else is bondage.

THREE-FOURTHS OF YOUR BIBLE

Now that we've discussed our freedom from a Sabbath day and a 10 percent tithe, an obvious question arises: Well, then, what use is the Old Testament? To begin to address this important question, we should keep in mind the following:

> *All Scripture* is God-breathed and is useful for teaching, rebuking, correcting and training in righteousness, so that all God's people may be thoroughly equipped for every good work.
>
> 2 TIMOTHY 3:16–17, italics added

I have made the argument that the law has no bearing on the life of the believer. But the Old Testament is a treasure that shouldn't be disregarded. In the Old Testament, we find out how the universe came into existence. We read of the fall of the human race. We learn why there's so much evil in the world. We experience the history of God's interactions with his people. We see his faithfulness despite their faithlessness. We see God's prophets at work and God's mercy on display. We learn about what God calls wisdom and how it differs from humans' sense of the same. We discover early indications of the coming Messiah, and we understand more fully how Jesus fulfilled prophecy.

The Old Testament offers us something we can't get from the New. It provides a thorough background in how God initiated a relationship with humankind and how we did whatever we could to ruin this relationship. The work of Christ has far greater impact against the backdrop of how despicably the human race has acted toward God. How gracious our God has been over the course of human history!

We also can't forget that the promise of the New has its root in the Old. God told Abraham that through his seed (Jesus), Abraham would be the father of many nations. The promise that salvation would come to many nations was given in the Old Testament long before the law.

To disregard the Old Testament is like covering up a huge portion of a portrait God has been painting for thousands of years. But it's important to read and teach from the Old Testament while keeping it in context.

In the Old Testament, we see God punishing the Israelites for their sins. In the New Testament, we see that God punished Jesus for our sins. In the Old Testament, we see God withdrawing his presence from his people. In the New Testament, we see that he'll never leave us or forsake us. Even a man after God's own heart, David, pleaded with God not to withdraw his Holy Spirit. David begged, "Do not cast me from your presence or take your Holy Spirit from me" (Psalm 51:11). We don't find such pleas from the apostles under the New.

> To disregard the Old Testament is like covering up a huge portion of a portrait God has been painting for thousands of years.

Life is radically different on this side of the cross — a truth we must recognize as we study the Old Testament. We read of dietary restrictions, yet we don't need to live by them. We read of ceremonial regulations, and we needn't abide by them. We read of requirements such as Sabbath observance and tithing, yet we're not bound by them. However, these restrictions, regulations, requirements, and commandments give us a fuller appreciation for what Jesus accomplished on our behalf.

10

THE STORY BEGAN IN A GARDEN WHEN A WOMAN TOOK A BITE FROM a piece of fruit offered by a serpent (Genesis 3:6). How obviously evil her goal was, right? Well, not really. The mistake we make is thinking that Eve was motivated by the desire to do evil. Nothing could be further from the truth. What she really wanted was to *avoid evil* and *do good*. In short, she wanted to do what God does — choose on her own, having the ability to detect evil and maintain goodness.

MORALITY TREE

Adam and Eve didn't eat from a "tree of evil." They ate from the tree of the *knowledge* of *good* and evil. Herein we see an important distinction. They weren't pursuing sin as we normally think of it. They were pursuing a form of godliness. They made an attempt to be like God. The serpent successfully lured them, and the bait was godlikeness. Even today, this is seen as a worthy goal.

But God never intended for humanity to take upon itself the burden of developing and following a code of ethics. The fall in the garden was due to Satan's cunning as he tempted the first humans to abandon God and choose human effort. Adam and Eve reconsidered their confidence in God's way and opted for morality instead. And desiring to fabricate their own system of right and wrong was their fatal mistake.

When we envision their taking a bite of the fruit, we'd like to ask Eve and Adam, "How could you do it? I mean, there was *only one thing* you weren't supposed to do, and you ruined it for all of us!" But what was their motive really? Although they were openly disobedient, we might say it was for a "right" reason. They wanted to be "right" and do "right." They wanted to know right from wrong so they could choose right and avoid wrong.

> Adam and Eve reconsidered their confidence in God's way and opted for morality instead.

How do we know they weren't interested in evil? The serpent's alluring statement was, "When you eat . . . your eyes will be opened, and you will be like God" (Genesis 3:5), and with that they were sunk. They admired God's goodness and desired to generate and exude that same quality. They had no interest in overtly evil pursuits. Had they ever even seen sinful behavior before?

The original sin was not Adam and Eve's thumbing their noses at the goodness of God. Instead, it was their wanting to author their own system of right and wrong so they could make *sure* they did right and avoided wrong. Today, we can be deceived by the same offer. We may find ourselves pursuing the knowledge of good instead of listening to our heartfelt yearning for an intimate relationship with Jesus Christ.

A DEATH-AND-LIFE ISSUE

Through the Eden story, we see our need for real life, not merely a set of instructions on how to live. But our need for life is not communicated through Genesis alone. It's amazing how certain words in the Scriptures begin to stick out once we're made aware of their meaning. Words like *life* and *death* leap off the page as we begin to see that Christianity isn't intended to meet humanity's ill-perceived need for religion. The real thing meets our deepest need in restoring to us genuine spiritual life.

> Christianity isn't intended to meet humanity's ill-perceived need for religion.

While some view Christianity as a behavior improvement program, the Eden story reveals that a desire for behavior improvement was the cause of spiritual death. Lack of moral laws isn't our problem. A plethora of socially and morally acceptable behavior improvement programs abound across world religions and even in many nonreligious movements. We could benefit from many of them if our primary need was merely a code of ethics to guide life choices.

Radically, the Bible teaches that humanity's main problem is not what we're doing. Instead, it's our *lack of life* as we do it. Paul describes our main problem in these ways:

> Just as sin entered the world through one man, and *death through sin*, and in this way *death came to all people*, because all sinned—
>
> ROMANS 5:12, italics added

> As for you, you were dead in your transgressions and sins.
>
> EPHESIANS 2:1

DIET FOR THE DEAD?

Imagine encountering a man's body lying by the side of the road. You decide to pull over to check the man's condition. As your car comes to a stop, you jump out and run toward him. Reaching down to check his pulse, you realize he has none. He's dead and gone, perhaps due to a heart attack. What can you do? Based on his appearance, you deduce that the man may have suffered heart failure due to a lifetime of poor eating habits. Instantly, you leap to your feet, rush to the car, pull out a diet book, and begin screaming important information from its pages as you head back toward him: "Chapter 1: Eating for Health and Heart!"

> No amount of education will change the heart of a spiritually dead person.

Stop to examine the absurdity of this situation. No amount of information on eating habits is going to resurrect this man. He's already dead. The only real solution would be for him to somehow obtain a new lease on life. In the same way, no amount of education will change the heart of a spiritually dead person. Life is the only solution to death:

> When you were dead in your sins and in the uncircumcision of your sinful nature [flesh], *God made you alive* with Christ.
>
> COLOSSIANS 2:13, italics added

> Because of his great love for us, God, who is rich in mercy, *made us alive* with Christ even when we were dead in transgressions—it is by grace you have been saved.
>
> EPHESIANS 2:4–5, italics added

God knew our real need. And through Christ he met that need by offering us life.* The law or any other system of morality could never offer us this life. Although some may think the law solves their problem, realistically it only brings more awareness of death. As we saw previously, the law isn't an encourager. Instead, it's a stern criticizer. The law makes one aware that there's

---

*See Sidelight 2 on pp. 229–30.

a serious problem at our core. Even after our concerted efforts to constrain behavior, the law is always present to condemn in one way or another.

The apostle Paul himself admits that he thought the law was the ultimate in spiritual experience. He was sorely disappointed to end up empty inside: "I found that the very commandment that was intended to bring life actually brought death" (Romans 7:10).

WHY DID JESUS DO THAT?

Why did Jesus seem to go out of his way to antagonize the Pharisees and other religious leaders? Why did he anger them throughout his ministry? He healed on the Sabbath, and they hated him for it. He turned over their money tables, and they despised him for it. He called them snakes, when doing so certainly didn't help the relationship. But he did these things to show the difference between real life and the counterfeit technique of self-focused behavior modification.

What had centuries of life under law produced in Jewish society by the time Jesus arrived on the scene? A Pharisee-led agenda that was worlds apart from Jesus' goal. While the Pharisees paraded through city streets condemning prostitutes and drunkards for their overtly sinful behavior, Jesus was befriending these same individuals. Jesus was gentle, merciful, and kind to sinners, while the Pharisees were harsh, judgmental, and rude to them.

> The law only breeds two things: defeat if you're honest and hypocrisy if you're not.

It appears that the only people who angered Jesus were the religious rulers of his day. Why? Because the law teachers were not being honest with themselves or others.

First, after watering down the potency of the law so as to

concoct a palatable mixture, they painted the illusion of spiritual success under law. Second, they added in their own regulations and beat their chests as they touted themselves as the spiritually elite. Jesus hated hypocrisy, and the law only breeds two things: defeat if you're honest and hypocrisy if you're not.

Through his resurrection, Jesus would eventually offer his Jewish contemporaries genuine life. The religious zealots of his day were working against him as they pretended to already possess life.

The source of life himself saw right through their charades.

PART 3

crossing the line

*The Cross is the central event in time and eternity,
and the answer to all the problems of both.*
Oswald Chambers (1874–1917)

11

IF YOU WERE TO PULL A "PRODIGAL SON" ROUTINE ON A PARENT, how do you think they would react? You may recall that the prodigal son asked for his inheritance early so he could enjoy life in the fast lane: "Dad, I was wondering if I might cash in on your will before you die?"

Good luck with that one today, right? It's just not done. You may end up with some cash in your hand, but it wouldn't be from the will. The attorneys would nip that in the bud. It's not legal to cash in on a will unless the author of the will is believed to be dead. Interestingly, this is a point made in Hebrews:

> In the case of a will, it is necessary to prove the death of the one who made it, because *a will is in force only when somebody has died*; it never takes effect while the one who made it is living.
>
> HEBREWS 9:16–17, italics added

Why all this talk about wills, the legal system, and inheritance? Here the writer is drawing an analogy between a will going into effect and a covenant taking effect. In fact, the terms *will, covenant,* and *testament* are translations of the same Greek word.

The writer's analogy and play on words serves to make an important point. Just as a will isn't in effect without a death, a covenant doesn't go into effect without a death. Meaning the New Covenant did not begin at Jesus' birth but at his death.

As you may imagine, this point carries radical implications. First, the New Testament doesn't actually begin in Matthew 1. In fact, it doesn't begin at any page in the Bible. It begins at the point in history when Jesus' blood was shed.

> The New Covenant did not begin at Jesus' birth but at his death.

No blood was shed in the first chapter of Matthew, and no sacrificial death was carried out in the manger. It was not our Savior's birth that changed everything. It was his death that inspired the apostles to declare the message of "out with the old, and in with the new."

As Paul puts it, Jesus was "born under the law, to redeem those under the law" (Galatians 4:4–5). So Jesus lived for thirty-three years on planet Earth while those around him still operated under the Old, not the New.*

Where should we look, then, to see the New? The first effects of the New are evidenced in the book of Acts at Pentecost.† The apostles' letters to the church instruct us about life under the New.

THE TRUE BEGINNING

When we attempt to mix Old with New, we end up with a contradictory covenant of our own invention. This is where I lived for years. Since there were a few elements of the New in my imaginary covenant, it didn't kill me right away. Instead, it afforded me a slower death.

I had adopted a belief system that was essentially a balance of Old and New. I neither suffered under the stringency of the entire law nor enjoyed the bliss of unconditional favor. For that reason,

---

*See Sidelight 3 on pp. 230–31. †See Sidelight 4 on pp. 231–32.

it would be years before my framework for relating to God would finally take its toll.

As you read this, you may be thinking, "Well, that's not my problem. I have never struggled with whether or not I am under the law. I've always known better." That may be true, but that was true for me too! I would never have said that I needed to adhere to the Jewish law—far from it. It wasn't the law of Moses that was holding me hostage; it was my own modern-day form of law that I was trying to live out.

Having raised my antennae toward the Christian world around me, I intercepted the subtle message that there are requirements to remain in God's favor. This collection of "Thou shalts"—read your Bible, share your faith, participate in a lot of "church"—was a measuring stick by which I determined my worth and standing. These criteria served as a concrete way of determining whether or not I was in right relationship with God.

> It was my own modern-day form of law that I was trying to live out.

I had already accepted the work of Christ as the means to heaven. But it was my approach to daily living that was beating me up. Law as an everyday operating system was doing its work.

SET ASIDE

If we're under a New Covenant, then what about the Old one? Is there still a place for it in our lives? What do the Scriptures say? Hebrews dismisses the notion of mingling the two:

> He *sets aside the first to establish the second.* And *by that will,* we have been made holy through the sacrifice of the body of Jesus Christ once for all.
>
> HEBREWS 10:9b–10, italics added

Through the New, we find our standing as holy children of God. The first (Old) covenant was set aside because it made no one perfect. After all, it was a performance-based system, and no one could perform in a way that met its standards! Imagine walking on eggshells your entire life as you try to do everything written in the law. How overwhelming! For that reason, the Old is now obsolete. It has been set aside due to our inability to cooperate with it:

> By calling this covenant "new," [God] has made the first one obsolete; and what is obsolete and outdated will soon disappear.
>
> HEBREWS 8:13

> The former regulation is set aside because it was weak and useless (for the law made nothing perfect), and a better hope is introduced, by which we draw near to God.
>
> HEBREWS 7:18–19

What does the writer of Hebrews say? The Old is "weak and useless" in its attempts to perfect us. Today, we have a better option—the New. This new system introduced through the death of Jesus Christ actually works. It places us in perfect standing even though we don't perform perfectly. Only through the New can we genuinely draw near to God.

When I'm feeling distant from God, it's because I've measured myself and have come up short. This leads me to believe that God must be measuring me by this same standard. So I end up with the false conclusion that he's distant from me. Under this logic, how would I get close again? Obviously, the only option would be to achieve in a way that I hadn't achieved previously.

But the Scriptures are clear: there's only one way to get close to God—through the New Covenant. Any other way is a counterfeit that is invariably rooted in ill-conceived parallels with human relationships and driven by moment-to-moment feelings.

12

Throughout the four gospels, Jesus talks about the law. So what does he say about it? And in what ways should Jesus' words affect how we apply the law today?

MAGNIFICATION AND MIRRORS

As a kid, I remember being fascinated by a mirror next to my mother's sink. It was a table-stand mirror that was round and double-sided. I could swivel the mirror to switch from standard reflection to a 3x magnification. After washing my face, I'd look into the standard reflection. My face would appear clean and clear. But once I flipped the mirror, the magnified side would reveal things I hadn't been able to see before. Flaws in my complexion that were previously concealed became highly visible in the magnified image.

Here are two examples of how Jesus spoke about the law. As you read his words, see if you can identify the ways in which he's magnifying the dirt on the face of humanity. Even the premium law keepers of the day appear filthy in light of what the law *really* requires:

> "You have heard that it was said to the people long
> ago, 'You shall not murder, and anyone who murders

will be subject to judgment.' *But I tell you* that anyone who is angry with a brother or sister will be subject to judgment."

MATTHEW 5:21–22, italics added

"You have heard that it was said, 'You shall not commit adultery.' *But I tell you* that anyone who looks at a woman lustfully has already committed adultery with her in his heart."

MATTHEW 5:27–28, italics added

What was Jesus doing when he spoke of the law? He was amplifying it, just as the double-sided mirror magnified the blemishes on my face. Jesus was using the law to show religious leaders exactly where they stood.

We often attempt to apply directly to our lives every word Jesus said, without considering his audience and purpose. But the context of Jesus' harsh teachings must be seen in the light of the dividing line between the Old and the New. Remember that Christ was born and lived during the Old Covenant (law) era:

But when the set time had fully come, God sent his Son, born of a woman, *born under the law, to redeem those under the law,* that we might receive adoption to sonship.

GALATIANS 4:4–5, italics added

Jesus was born under the law. His audience was under the law. And they needed deliverance from it. So what would Jesus teach about the current religious system? Would he praise his hearers for their performance? Would he leave them satisfied with the status quo? Or would he highlight their feeble attempts at keeping the law? Naturally, he'd do the latter. Otherwise, what use would his work on the cross be to them?

> Jesus' audience was under the law.

So Jesus exposed the futility of life under law. He exclaimed, "Gouge out your eye" and "cut off your hand" if you truly want to keep the law (Matthew 5:29–30), so that his Jewish listeners would reach a crossroad. They would decide to try harder or to give up.

Which response do you think Jesus was hoping for as he swiveled the mirror so they could see their dirty faces in magnified form?

Once they gave up, they could consider a radical new way.

Jesus' real intent might be most clear in the story of the rich young man. This man had tried his best to keep the law. Jesus looked at him and loved him. So why would Jesus point to the one thing this young man *couldn't* do? Why would Jesus send him away brokenhearted?

> "Teacher," [the man] declared, "all these [commandments] I have kept since I was a boy."
>
> Jesus looked at him and loved him. "One thing you lack," he said. "Go, sell everything you have and give to the poor, and you will have treasure in heaven. Then come, follow me."
>
> At this the man's face fell. He went away sad, because he had great wealth.
>
> MARK 10:20–22

Should we put our possessions on eBay in order to enter the kingdom? Jesus said we should, didn't he? But this simply doesn't jibe with New Testament teachings on salvation through faith alone. Jesus' impossible teachings of "sell everything, sever body parts if necessary, be perfect like God and surpass the Pharisees with your righteousness" are not *honestly* compatible with salvation as a gift from God.

Jesus was teaching hopelessness under the Old.

Couldn't we resolve all of this by realizing the dividing line in human history? Peter, James, John, and Paul wrote epistles about life under the New Covenant. Years earlier, Jesus was teaching hopelessness under the Old. The audience wasn't the same. The covenant wasn't the same. And the teachings aren't the same.

KILLER SERMON

Barbara had been struggling with depression for more than a decade. Painful circumstances had overwhelmed her to the point where she had little hope. One day, she was watching television when our church's half-hour program came on. Barbara listened as I told of my own battle with guilt and anxiety over performing for God.

Barbara's struggle was so similar that she decided to call me. After we had talked together just a couple of times, Barbara began to notice some change. There was a difference in the way she felt about herself, in her perception of God, and in her overall energy level as she made her way through her day.

Barbara shared with me that reading the Bible had always been discouraging to her. There was always *more to do* that she wasn't doing. "Every time I picked up the Bible, I felt like a failure," she said.

Lately though, all of that had changed. We had examined a few dozen Scripture passages about her identity in Christ, her freedom from the law's demands, and the boundless forgiveness she has in Christ. She told me that when she set her mind on those truths, she began to experience some relief from her debilitating depression.

But one evening, Barbara came into my office with a downcast expression again. "What happened?" I asked.

"Well, everything was fine most of the week as I was reading the verses you gave me," she said. "But then I decided to read Jesus' Sermon on the Mount. After that, I'm not sure what happened."

"Ah, I see," I responded. "Let me assure you that what you experienced is normal for any honest, eager child of God when they read that passage."

I explained the dividing line of Old and New. I told her how Jesus' harsh teachings aimed at the religious kill you every time. Barbara began to see the distinction between what Jesus taught to Jews and what God wanted her to enjoy under the New. Her countenance lifted. Once again, truth had done its work.

> Jesus' harsh teachings aimed at the religious kill you every time.

One thing about distinguishing the Old from the New — it always liberates.

13

ALTHOUGH SOME CLAIM WE'RE OBLIGATED TO KEEP THE LAW OR portions of it, Paul doesn't mince words about the issue: *"Christ is the end of the law* so that there may be righteousness for everyone who believes" (Romans 10:4 NIV, italics added). But substituting rules for the work of the Spirit is not a new phenomenon. Nearly two thousand years ago, Paul was outraged at believers whom he had personally taught. They were straying from the simple message of "Jesus plus nothing." Filled with emotion, he begged them to reconsider their position:

> You foolish Galatians! Who has bewitched you? Before your very eyes Jesus Christ was clearly portrayed as crucified. I would like to learn just one thing from you: Did you receive the Spirit by observing the law, or by believing what you heard? Are you so foolish? After beginning with the Spirit, are you now trying to finish by human effort?
>
> GALATIANS 3:1–3

Later in the same chapter, Paul clarifies the believer's relationship to the law: "The law was put in charge to lead us to Christ that we might be justified by faith. Now that faith has come, we are no longer under the supervision of the law" (Galatians 3:24–25 NIV).

The law led us to Christ. How? By acting as a yardstick against which we measured our morality. We came up short. God's solution was to justify us, to declare us righteous, by Christ's work. So Paul asks us to consider the following: First, how did we receive the Spirit—through believing or through the law? Second, what should supervise our actions now?

> The law led us to Christ.

MULTIPLE CHOICE

In college, I was relieved when professors chose the multiple-choice format for tests. Even without studying, I had a fighting chance of identifying the correct answer. In Galatians, the apostle is quizzing his readers on their years of learning under his teaching. He takes it easy on them by giving them multiple-choice options.

If Paul were to rewrite this portion of his letter in test format, it might look like the following:

Question 1: How were you saved?

☐ by observing the law

☐ by believing what I heard

Question 2: How do you expect to grow?

☐ by my human effort

☐ by the Spirit

Using this line of questioning, Paul is urging Christians to continue *in the same way they began*. They started by believing and by opening themselves to the Spirit's work. Salvation had nothing to do with the law. Likewise, maturity in Christ isn't achieved through human effort either.

Paul emphasizes that the law should not act as our supervisor. Is Paul referring here to salvation or to daily living? Both. First, we're saved by hearing with faith. Now that we're saved, our daily lives are carried out by faith in the indwelling Christ, not by the law. The Spirit within us is more than enough to bring about a life the law never could: "If you are led by the Spirit, you are not under the law" (Galatians 5:18).

> Our daily lives are carried out by faith in the indwelling Christ, not by the law.

THE SECRET FORMULA

So if the Scriptures say that the law has no place in the life of the believer, the most logical question is this: If the law isn't our moral guide, then what is? As Christians, we have an inborn desire for our behavior to turn out right. In fact, the desire to please God is what drives some to embrace the error of law-based living!

Fortunately, God hasn't taken us out from under the law and left us with nothing. When we believe, the Holy Spirit then lives in us. The Spirit produces fruit through us as we depend on him. But it's important to recognize the "system" that the Holy Spirit uses in place of the law. He operates through a radically different system, namely, one called *grace*. Recognizing the work of the Holy Spirit in our lives requires a solid understanding of grace.

But often our idea of grace boils down to nothing more than mercy. In this case, the typical definition of *grace* might go something like this: "Grace is what happens when a punishment is lessened or waived after someone has done wrong." Grace is often seen as a response to sin, much like being pardoned from a capital crime.

But the New Testament portrays grace as far greater than this. Notice what grace does in the lives of Christians:

> *The grace of God* has appeared that offers salvation to all people. *It teaches us to say "No" to ungodliness* and worldly passions, and to live self-controlled, upright and godly lives in this present age.
>
> TITUS 2:11–12, italics added

Grace is the system that the Holy Spirit uses to counsel and teach us on a daily basis. Grace is in place, whether or not we've sinned recently. We worry that an absence of law will result in a lifestyle that is out of control. This concern is natural. But it contradicts what the Scriptures say about the effects of grace. Grace isn't just a treatment for sin; it's actually the cure for sin!

When we question the function of grace in our lives, we're insulting God's intelligence. Would he usher in a New Covenant that not only allows but actually promotes sin? Is God foolish to think that grace really motivates us to live godly lives?

The secret is that grace deactivates our pride. Removing the law from our lives means our self-effort is no longer prodded to control behavior. The law excites human effort. It encourages us to depend on resources outside of Christ. But unconditional acceptance deactivates human effort and allows the Holy Spirit to be all that he wants to be through us.

The law excites human effort.

Our greatest fear is that we'll be out of control. But we were never made to be in control. Self-control has always been a natural attribute of *the Holy Spirit*. The reason he lives within us is to produce the self-control that we're afraid we'll lack under grace.

Paul encourages us to trust grace under the New Covenant by quoting Jesus himself on the matter:

But [Jesus] said to me, "My grace is sufficient for you, for my power is made perfect in weakness." Therefore I will boast all the more gladly about my weaknesses, so that Christ's power may rest on me.

2 CORINTHIANS 12:9

Jesus doesn't appear fearful about the outcome of too much grace in Paul's life. Grace isn't merely a response to sin. Grace is the core of the New. It allows Jesus to produce through us what's needed in the moment. After hearing this divine position on grace, Paul decides that Someone greater than himself will work in his life. Jesus will produce what he cannot.

The same is true for us today.

PRISON BREAK

Long-term prisoners often struggle after their release. They grew accustomed to the confines of prison. In some ways, walls and bars provided a sense of security for them. They were told when to shower, when to eat, when to exercise, and when to sleep. Every aspect of their lives was regulated as law enforcers kept a watchful eye.

Once released, some grow uneasy. Suddenly, they must figure out for themselves where to go, when to do things, and what to do with the rest of their lives.

"It is for freedom that Christ has set us free" (Galatians 5:1).

Similarly, freedom from the law can make some of us uneasy.* When boundaries are removed, we're left to make up our minds concerning what is and what isn't profitable. But this is what Christian maturity is: since we're in Christ and he's in us, we don't look to external rules to determine our every

---

*See Sidelight 5 on pp. 232–33.

move; instead, we're urged to move away from religious bondage and to journey toward a beautiful freedom, never looking back:

> It is for freedom that Christ has set us free. Stand firm, then, and do not let yourselves be burdened again by a yoke of slavery.
>
> GALATIANS 5:1

PART 4

burning matryoshkas

Do not let us consider ourselves as far off when
God has made us one with him.

Hudson Taylor (1832–1905)

14

HOW MANY SINS DOES IT TAKE TO BECOME A SINNER?

This is a question I pose during our "Naked Gospel" seminar. And I usually watch a majority of the audience mouthing the word *one*. "It only takes *one* sin to become a sinner," they say. The reality, however, is that it takes none — zero.

We're *born* sinners.

I know what you're thinking. That was a trick question. It may be, but the common answer to this question reveals what the average person believes about nature. *Human* nature. When we buy the idea that it takes one sin to become a sinner, we assume the following:

- We *do* in order to *be*.
- We presume that doing precedes being.
- Hence, people *become* sinners or *become* saints by doing things that sinners or saints do.

But is this biblical? I don't think it is, and as a result it hinders the unbeliever from understanding their fallen nature by birth. It also hinders the believer from comprehending their new nature by re-birth. But if we can grasp that by birth we're sinners, only then can we see how by birth alone — our new birth — we become saints.

Saints by Birth

In a heartbeat, Christians buy the idea that the world is full of sinners. Once enlightened by the Scriptures, we also agree that we're born in a sinful condition. Perhaps because spiritual death is a lowly state, we easily agree that the world is fallen. But when it comes to believing that we're 100 percent righteous by *re*birth, we stutter and stammer over our words. In short, we believers consent to "birth determines identity" for the world but not for our own selves.

Within the Catholic vein of thought, saints are those who have suffered for the gospel. They've performed miracles and supposedly achieved a higher moral state than the average Joe or Jane. Within Protestant thinking, *saint* isn't often used to describe an individual Christian. We appear more comfortable with the terms *believer*, *Christian*, or *saved person*. In fact, we'd even describe ourselves as *sinners*, although we're quick to tack on the phrase *saved by grace*.

The term *saint* (meaning "holy one" or "one reserved, set apart, for God") is hard to swallow for many. Likewise, to actually use the term *righteous* to describe ourselves is sometimes seen as the epitome of arrogance. But these are precisely the terms that God uses to describe those who are in Christ. How can he be comfortable using these words while being fully aware of our shortcomings and failures? To answer this question, we have to take a deeper look at the idea that birth determines identity. And along the way I think we'll discover some amazing things about who we are.

> Birth determines identity.

Rectors and Farleys

In my growing-up days, we lived on a horse farm in northern Virginia. And we only had one close neighbor, the Rectors. There were four boys in the Rector family, and I really enjoyed spending time with them. We'd ride horses, go fishing, and race around the farm on ATVs.

Two Rector boys were older than I was, and I looked up to them. They were cool, and I felt privileged to tag along with them wherever they went. I found myself dressing like the Rectors, combing my hair like them, even talking and acting like them. Nearly every day, I'd go over to their house, eat lunch with them, play with their dog, Skipper, and throw the football in their yard. It *felt* as though I were a Rector.

Reality would set in, however, any time there was a family reunion or gathering. I wouldn't get an invitation. Although I could look, talk, and act like a Rector, I wasn't a Rector by birth. My birth certificate will always say *Farley*. Even if I were to somehow arrange for adoption as a Rector, I wouldn't really be a member of the Rector bloodline. Why? Because birth determines identity.

You can probably see the parallel with our spiritual identity. When we show up on planet Earth, our birth certificate reads *Adam's family*. Not to be confused with the wardrobe-challenged family from TV, *Adam's family* here means we're born in Adam. Because of our natural birth into his bloodline, we're spiritually dead by birth and by nature.

The fall of Adam and Eve occurred *before* they gave birth to Cain, Abel, Seth, and other children. So just as Cain had Dad's nose and Abel had Mom's eyes, the kids also inherited *spiritual* genetics. The long-term result was a race of humans who were spiritually dead at birth, beginning with the very first descendants.

No matter what we do, we cannot make ourselves spiritually alive, any more than I could make myself a Rector. We can bring about reform in our behavior, but no effort of any kind will remove us from Adam's spiritual bloodline and place us in Christ's.

IMAGE IS EVERYTHING

Although Adam himself was created in God's image, Genesis reveals that Adam's children were born in Adam's own image:

> When God created man, he made him in the likeness of God. He created them male and female and blessed them. And when they were created, he called them "man."
>
> When Adam had lived 130 years, he had a son *in his own likeness, in his own image.*
>
> GENESIS 5:1–3 NIV, italics added

The contrast here seems clear. Adam was made in the likeness of God, but Adam's son was born in Adam's own likeness. And then the writer repeats: *in his own image.* So according to Scripture, are we born in the image of God? It's true that, after salvation, we are re-created in Christ Jesus and are being renewed in his image (Colossians 3:10). But originally, we are descended from Adam, the first man.

At birth, we bear *Adam's* image.

> Are we *born* in the image of God?

Earlier, I asked how many sins it takes to become a sinner. The answer is *zero*, since we're born as sinners. But in a sense, it does take one sin for us to become sinners. However, that one sin was not committed by us. Romans 5 reveals that one man's sin brought the following effects:

- sin entered the world (verse 12)
- the many died (verse 15)
- condemnation came on all people (verse 18)
- the many were made sinners (verse 19)

Adam's spiritual death caused all of his descendants to be born spiritually dead. Adam's sin brought condemnation on us all. And Adam's sin earned each of us the title *sinner.* Our spiritual state stems from *our lineage in Adam*, not from what we individually are doing.

Just as I imitated the Rector family, I could try to imitate Jesus Christ for the rest of my life. But even the most rigid conformity to Christ-like behavior wouldn't place me in his spiritual bloodline. I am who I am by birth, not by behavior.

Realizing that it's all about birth, not behavior, is illuminating. It brings new meaning to that often misused and even abused term *born again*. This phrase is so frequently uttered that many have lost sight of its true meaning; however, in light of our spiritual bloodline at birth, we can understand why Jesus used the term.

Jesus told Nicodemus that each human being's real need is to be born a second time. He wasn't urging the Jewish leader to turn over a new leaf, to try harder, or to polish his lifestyle. Instead, he was addressing the heart of the matter, namely, birth. While some regard Christianity as a behavior improvement program dressed up in religious clothing, Jesus revealed that God's plan was actually an exchange of nature.

> God's plan was actually an exchange of nature.

The Verdict Is "In"

Since our problem stems from lineage, the solution also relates to lineage. If we are in Adam at birth, we must be in Someone else for genuine change to occur: "As *in Adam* all die, so *in Christ* all will be made alive" (1 Corinthians 15:22, italics added).

Everyone is *in* someone spiritually. When a person becomes a Christian, he or she isn't simply adopting certain doctrines. Nor is he or she merely being awarded entrance into heaven. On the very day that someone places faith in the work of Christ, he or she undergoes surgery. He may not comprehend it; she may not feel it. But although the surgery is spiritual, it's no less real than a medical procedure.

At salvation, we're hoisted out of the lifeline of Adam and transferred into the lifeline of Christ. Our spiritually dead DNA is miraculously extracted, and new, living DNA is inserted into our spirits. We become part of a new family.

> New, living DNA is inserted into our spirits.

We're no longer *in* the flesh.

We're *in* the Spirit.

This surgery carries all kinds of implications for who we really are, what we're designed for, and what fulfills us at the deepest level of personhood.

15

MANY YEARS AGO, MY MOTHER COLLECTED RUSSIAN MATRYOSHKA dolls. If you're familiar with these dolls, you know there's more to them than meets the eye. Made of wood, these dolls are cut across the middle so that when you pull off the top half, it opens to reveal a smaller doll inside. When you take out and open the next doll, you find an even smaller doll inside. This continues, of course, until the last, smallest doll is revealed. Looking at the largest doll from the outside, you'd never guess what's inside.

Because each doll is inside a larger doll, what happens to one doll happens to the others. If you lift the doll up and place it on a shelf, all the other dolls inside are raised up as well. If you dispose of the doll in a fire, the dolls inside are also burned.

Matryoshka dolls help me understand what it means to be *in* Christ. The Bible tells us that we're "hidden with Christ in God" (Colossians 3:3). I imagine most of us don't think much about what it means to be hidden in God. But the Scriptures emphasize our being *in* Christ about six times more often than the fact that Christ is in us. Obviously, this is an important truth that God wants us to grasp.

> Most of us don't think much about what it means to be hidden in God.

Paul tells the Corinthians and the Colossians of this spiritual transfer of our selves into Christ:

> It is because of [God] that you are *in Christ Jesus*, who has become for us wisdom from God—that is, our righteousness, holiness and redemption.
>
> 1 CORINTHIANS 1:30, italics added

> He rescued us from the domain of darkness, and transferred us to the kingdom of His beloved Son.
>
> COLOSSIANS 1:13 NASB

It was God who changed our spiritual location. He transported us from a position in Adam to a place within Christ. Because of our original position in Adam, we were like Adam. Through our new location in Christ, we become like Christ. We are spiritually alive and righteous.

So how exactly did we leave behind who we used to be and become so different on the inside? Let's turn our attention to the surgery that forever changed our spiritual DNA.

YOUR OWN FUNERAL

We're acquainted with the crucifixion and burial of Jesus Christ. After all, they're historical events. But it's an altogether different matter to realize that *we ourselves* were spiritually crucified and buried with him.

> *We ourselves* were spiritually crucified and buried with him.

The moment we enter into Christ at salvation, our old self is obliterated. This takes place as God kills off the old self through a miraculous, timeless surgery. We're crucified with Christ:

> Don't you know that all of us who were baptized into
> Christ Jesus were baptized into his death? We were there-
> fore buried with him through baptism into death. . . .
> For we know that *our old self was crucified with him* . . .
>
> ROMANS 6:3–4a, 6a, italics added

As amazing as it is to be crucified with Christ, it's not enough!
God goes further as he resurrects us from the dead and seats us at
his right hand with Christ: "God *raised us up with Christ* and seated
us with him in the heavenly realms in Christ Jesus" (Ephesians
2:6, italics added).

For a short time, Jesus Christ walked as one of us in the likeness of sinful flesh. But today he's seated in heaven with God. And
we're joined to him! We're not merely joined to the earth-walking
Messiah who was temporarily lower than the angels. We're joined
to the *risen* Christ.

Sometimes we see ourselves as sinners in the loving arms of
a God who is pretending not to see us as we really are. In our
minds, maybe God is wearing a pair of "Jesus glasses" that hides
our true state from his vision. We find it difficult to grasp the idea
that God calls us righteous *because
we actually are righteous*. It feels more
humble to believe that we're filthy
worms awaiting a future change into
beautiful butterflies.

> If we Christians
> don't claim to possess
> perfect righteousness,
> we're lowering
> God's standard.

Jesus stated it best. He said that
our righteousness must surpass that
of the Pharisees in order to enter
the kingdom (Matthew 5:20). So if we Christians don't claim
to possess perfect righteousness, we're lowering God's standard.
We're watering down the gospel. We insinuate that Jesus can
unite himself with sin. And we insult the perfection of God.

Only perfection will do. This is precisely why God had to make us perfectly righteous in our human spirits through our own death, burial, and resurrection. With its apparent humility, this filthy worm theology appeals to the flesh. But God certainly doesn't condone our wallowing in a poor self-image.

The risen Christ doesn't join himself to filthy worms. The *Holy* Spirit doesn't dwell in dirty sinners. Christ only unites himself with those who are like him in spirit. The Holy Spirit doesn't reside in someone who remains even 1 percent flawed by sin.

But we've been perfectly cleansed. And we've been made perfectly righteous at our core through spiritual surgery. This is the only way we can enjoy even a moment of relationship with Jesus Christ.

THE CORE

Some see Christianity as a movement or campaign. We observe people behaving according to certain patterns and influencing others to do the same. In some ways, we fail to acknowledge that the gospel isn't *centrally* about behavior modification. At its core, the true message is about dying and miraculously being resurrected into a new person.

Sure, life in Christ has implications for behavior. But we can't afford to miss the *death* and *life* issues because we're obsessed with the effects rather than the cause. Describing the core of the message, Paul writes the following:

> For you died, and your life is now hidden with Christ in God. When Christ, who is your life, appears, then you also will appear with him in glory.
>
> COLOSSIANS 3:3–4

COMMUNICATING THE CORE

In college, a friend and I went around in circles for hours as we discussed issues such as grace and faith. For some reason, we simply couldn't see eye to eye on spiritual matters.

After we had carried on for some time, I finally said, "I don't really know how to explain it. But the real thing isn't about trying hard to act differently. Becoming a Christian is like dying and waking up the next day as a totally new person." With those words, we ended the conversation. A short time later, I headed to Greece and Italy for a study-abroad program and didn't see my friend for nearly six months.

A few days after my return to campus, my friend approached me and said, "Hey, I finally understood what you meant."

"Meant about what?" I asked, having forgotten about our conversation.

"You know, about dying and becoming a new person. One night, I began thinking about how you had described things. So I prayed and asked God to kill me and make me a new person."

"God, kill me" isn't your typical salvation prayer. But for six months, the words I had selected out of sheer desperation had remained with my friend. And one day he chose to act on them. In the end, it wasn't any of my fine-tuned and carefully honed arguments that penetrated my friend's heart. It was one central truth—the need to die and become new. This was his most pressing need, and this was what God used to reach him.

> "God, kill me" isn't your typical salvation prayer.

Death and new life are at the core of the gospel.

IT'S REAL

People who place their faith in Christ undergo a miraculous exchange at the center of their being. Who they were in Adam is no longer there. They become a new person, a child of God who is *in* Christ.

The key event causing this exchange is a death, burial, and resurrection with Christ. This miraculous exchange is not figurative or symbolic but *literal* and *actual*. The spiritual part of every Christian has *literally* and *actually* been crucified, buried, and raised with Christ. The fact that this occurs spiritually (and not physically) doesn't make it any less real.

> The old self is entirely obliterated.

So what happens to the old self that was in Adam? Once a person is in Christ, the old self is entirely obliterated. Therefore, an obvious question arises: *If my old self is dead and gone, why do I still sin?*

This isn't a new question. Believers in the early church asked the same thing. Thankfully, the same apostle who informs us that our old self is dead also provides solid answers about why we still struggle with sin.

16

THE SHOCKING AND LIBERATING REVELATION OF THE NEW SELF really happens when we can explain why we still struggle with sin. Throughout history we have taken up creative and often impressive mental gymnastics in our attempts to reconcile these two scriptural ideas: (1) the old self is dead, but (2) we still sin.

Many have held to the idea that the old self is only *positionally dead* or is *progressively dying* over time. But the same epistles that claim Jesus solved our *behavior* problem by dying on the cross and taking our sins away also state that Jesus solved our *identity* problem by giving us a new heart, a new spirit, and God's Spirit. We accept forgiveness as actual, Jesus' own death as actual, heaven as actual, and Jesus' return as actual. We don't have the right to relegate the death of our old self to the realm of the positional or the progressive.

I believe that Romans 6, for example, should be read in the same way we read the rest of the epistle—in a literal sense. Of course, if this is true, then we must find some real answers to the following question: If the death of my old self is literal, actual, and final, why then do I still end up sinning?

Why do I still end up sinning?

THE BATTLE WITHIN

Before we continue, ponder an important question: If we find a satisfactory answer to why we still struggle with sin, can we finally believe that our old self is dead, buried, and gone, that no portion of our old self is still present within us? My heart's desire is that you know the purity of who you are as a new creation, and that at the same time you are able to explain your ongoing struggle with sin. If we grasp these two realities, we'll be equipped to approach daily life and temptation as God intended.

We will start with the premise that knowing the *source* of temptation is valuable in resisting temptation. If you've ever tried to resist your own desires, you know how difficult resisting can be. For example, in an effort to avoid the pain of unreciprocated love, you try not to love someone. Still, your heart cries out for them. You can't just pretend that your love doesn't exist. Or you want to lose weight, and you try to resist your appetite for a favorite treat.

If resisting sin means saying no to what *we* truly desire, then our quest for victory over temptation will fail. But fortunately this isn't the picture that God paints for us. Instead, he reveals an entity called *the flesh* that works to prevent us from doing what we truly desire.

LOST IN TRANSLATION

Right away, we must differentiate the term *flesh* from the term *sinful nature*. The Greek word used in the original manuscripts is *sarx*, which is literally translated as "flesh." This is how *sarx* is translated in the New American Standard Bible and in many other English translations. However, one popular English translation, the New International Version, translates *sarx* by using the phrase *sinful nature* instead (putting *flesh* in the text note).

The phrase *sinful nature* can lead to inaccurate and harmful ideas about the new heart, mind, and spirit that we have in Christ. There's nothing within the Greek word *sarx* that connotes "sinful" or "nature." The NIV rendition is an expansion of the term.

The NIV is a wonderful English translation that makes ideas accessible to the average reader. In nearly all cases, there's no harm done as translators expound on the Greek to make the English as accurate, clear, and readable as possible. But in this particular case, the attempt to make God's Word more understandable has actually led to some misunderstanding.

As a result, many Christians today believe that their constant, ongoing struggle is with the sinful nature and, more precisely, *their* sinful nature. It's not much of a stretch to go from (1) *I have a sinful nature* to (2) *I am a sinner by nature* to (3) *The most natural thing for me to do is sin*. Then we wrongly conclude that who we are (our nature) at the very core is sinful, when in fact the Scriptures teach just the opposite. We are now partakers of God's divine nature (2 Peter 1:4)!

> We wrongly conclude that who we are (our nature) at the very core is sinful.

Our struggle as Christians is against something called *the flesh*, not against our own nature. The whole point of the gospel is that Jesus Christ has made each of us who believe into a new person. The old has gone, and the new has come. To deny this or to water it down is to miss the potency of the message altogether.

But given the radical claims about our personhood, it's essential to examine the Scriptures to better understand what the flesh is and how it operates.

FLESHLY IDENTITY

The first thing we see about the flesh is that it can serve as a resource from which we gain a sense of wisdom, strength, and status: "Consider your calling, brethren, that there were not many wise according to the flesh, not many mighty, not many noble" (1 Corinthians 1:26 NASB).

Smart. Strong. Popular. The flesh wishes to provide a sense of identity rooted in intellectual attributes, physical characteristics, or social status. The flesh wants us to gain identity from the *soul* (mind or intellect) or the *body* (family lineage or physical appearance) as opposed to the *spirit*—our new identity in Christ.

Growing up in the Washington, D.C., area, I knew individuals who built their identity around politics. In academia, there's the temptation to build identity around job titles and intellectual accomplishments. In Hollywood, some think they should be treated like nobility because of their fame and wealth. Still others spend their lives grooming their physical appearance, because to them it's a source of value and worth.

Confidence in the flesh is a choice.

Whether we seek our identity through intellect, social status, or physical appearance makes no difference. It's all a pursuit of identity and fulfillment according to the flesh.

So far, we might define *flesh* as "an approach to gaining a respected, strong, or popular identity in this world." Paul's rhetoric backs this up:

> If anyone else has a mind to put confidence in the flesh, I far more: circumcised the eighth day, of the nation of Israel, of the tribe of Benjamin, a Hebrew of Hebrews; as to the Law, a Pharisee; as to zeal, a persecutor of the church; as to the righteousness which is in the Law, found blameless.
>
> PHILIPPIANS 3:4–6 NASB

Confidence in the flesh is a choice. We can choose to build an identity around our birth into a certain family or our accomplishments. In Paul's case, he constructed a positive self-image using his Club Israel membership card (circumcision), his nationality, his tribe, his religious achievements, and his reputation. After all was said and done, Paul concluded that the identity he had built for himself was worthless. He discovered that bragging about heritage, lineage, and religiosity was pitiful next to knowing a real identity *in Jesus Christ.*

THE FLIP SIDE

When we think of the term *flesh*, we tend to envision bad-looking traits being produced in one's life—gossiping, lusting, and other ugly manifestations of sin. Although the Bible cites these as deeds of the flesh, there's a flip side. Sure, the flesh is delighted to coerce us toward obvious evil. But the flesh is equally satisfied to initiate religious or moral living admired by others!

Don't believe for a minute that the flesh is limited in its scope to producing ugly behavior. The flesh will build *any* kind of identity, as long as it gains love, attention, and acceptance from someone. As you read Paul's question directed to the Galatians, see if you can identify the "type" of flesh at work in their lives: "Are you so foolish? Having begun by the Spirit, are you now being *perfected by the flesh?*" (Galatians 3:3 NASB, italics added).

The flesh wasn't trying to produce evil-looking behavior in the Galatians. Instead, these Christians were employing fleshly effort as a means of *perfecting themselves* (growing) in Christ! They regarded their smarts and moral fortitude as the route to spiritual maturity.

Are we any less off course today?

We're intended to grow in the same way that we first received Christ—through dependency on him. There's no substitute for his work in our lives. A flesh-based method of self-improvement may appeal if we're not informed about God's way to maturity.

But God's way is simple and straightforward: Jesus plus nothing! As Paul writes, "I am confident of this very thing, that [God] who began a good work in you will perfect it until the day of Christ Jesus" (Philippians 1:6 NASB).

A DEFINITION

Through these and other Bible passages about the goals and cravings of the flesh, we glean some important facts:

- The flesh is a way to *think*.
- The flesh is a way to *walk*.
- The flesh *works against* the Spirit.
- The flesh encourages *self-effort*.
- The flesh seeks *identity* and *purpose*.
- We choose to *put confidence in* the flesh.

But the flesh is not the old self. It's something that is with us, but it's not us. We choose to depend on the flesh (or the Spirit) in any given moment. The choices we make depend on whether we recognize the agenda of the flesh and the futility of its ways.

> The flesh is not the old self.

Our poor choices to live according to the flesh are not any indication of our nature. Christians are new creations at heart, no matter how we choose to walk in a given moment. Christians are *in* the Spirit. But we choose to walk after the Spirit or after the flesh as circumstances hit us.

BEING YOURSELF

Have you ever pretended to be someone you're not? Maybe to impress someone else, you gave the impression that you were more than you actually were. It's all too possible to act in a way that's inconsistent with who we are. And we usually do so when we're concerned with what someone else may think.

When we walk after the flesh, *we're not being ourselves.* If we rely on intellect, strength, or physical appearance to gain purpose and fulfillment, we're walking after the flesh. But again, this is no indication of our nature. In fact, depending on the flesh goes *against* our nature.

We're designed for dependency on Christ. Walking after the Spirit is our destiny. We'll never be content with walking after the flesh or fashioning an identity outside of Christ. We can do it, but it won't fulfill.

Before we were in Christ, we had no choice but to gain identity and a sense of fulfillment from the flesh.

> Being yourself and expressing Christ are one and the same.

But now, as children of God, there's a battle within us. When we walk after the flesh, the Holy Spirit and our new human spirit (the new self) cry out to be heard.

Living a life of dependency on the Spirit is really nothing more than being ourselves. We were built for it from the ground up. After all, we are now God's workmanship (Ephesians 2:10). We're designed for walking in the attitudes and actions that God has already prepared for us.

For a Christian, because of your new identity in Christ, being yourself and expressing Christ are one and the same. God has arranged it so that our new self and our union with his Spirit cause us to want what he wants. God has the market cornered on true fulfillment. And he has installed within us an intense and never-ending desire to find fulfillment through expressing his life.

17

UNFORTUNATELY, THE FLESH ISN'T ON ITS OWN. IT HAS A POWERFUL ally whose agenda is to distract us from walking after the Spirit. Who is this ally? A power at work in us called *sin*.

SIN, NOT SINS

First, we must distinguish *sin* from the plural *sins*. Of course, *sins* are attitudes or behaviors we engage in. But *sin* is altogether different.

Here's the very first reference to *sin*, which occurs in Genesis as God speaks with Cain: "Sin is crouching at your door; it desires to have you, but you must rule over it" (Genesis 4:7). Here, God warns Cain about an imminent threat. Within the warning, God reveals an important concept that applies to us today. There's a power called *sin*, and its desire is to overtake us.

Again, we're not speaking of *sins* or *sinning* but of an entity called *sin*. God doesn't warn Cain about sinful behavior. Instead, he's concerned about an organized force complete with desires and an agenda to control.

A battle is taking place right under our noses. We know we're being tempted, but how should we understand the source of those urges? The apostle Paul recounts his battle as he tried to live as a

Pharisee under the demands of the law. In Romans 7:14, he announces his own personal discovery that he was "unspiritual, sold as a slave to sin." While under the law, Saul of Tarsus first thought he had it all together. Until sin had its way with him, he had no idea that he was living in slavery. God used the law to give Saul a deep sense of his sinfulness. Later, God used the Damascus Road experience to deliver him from spiritual slavery.

Saul of Tarsus experienced a startling revelation, one that can dramatically alter the way we view our thought lives today. An organized and person-like power called *sin* was at work *in* Saul, causing him to do things that he didn't intend to do. This force was not Saul himself. It was something other than Saul, although it was acting through his physical body. Take careful note of the words used to describe Saul's struggle with sin while under the Jewish law:

> Sin is an organized force complete with desires and an agenda to control.

> I do not understand what I do. For what I want to do I do not do, but what I hate I do. And if I do what I do not want to do, I agree that the law is good. As it is, it is *no longer I myself who do it*, but it is *sin* living in me.
>
> ROMANS 7:15–17, italics added

Notice that Saul places the blame on something that was *not* him. Wow! Here we see that sinful thoughts were served up from a secondary source called *sin*. Sin lived *in* Saul, but sin was *not* Saul.

Is this force called *sin* still active? And is it still housed in the physical bodies of Christians today? Absolutely. At salvation, nothing happened to the power of sin. It is still alive and at work in our bodies. After all, the power of sin didn't get saved; *we* did! And we won't have new bodies until we hit heaven. So the presence of sin within our bodies won't change until then.

What if Christians today recognized that their bodies house a nagging force that acts *in* them and may even feel *like* them but is *not* them? What would it mean for you to understand your struggle in this way?

But today we are often willing, even eager, to state that we're sinful like everyone else. We think we're being humble to claim that we're no better than anyone else in the world around us.

But the New Testament paints a very different picture.

Apparently, we're aliens in this world, and our citizenship is elsewhere.

> Christians today are willing, even eager, to state that we're sinful like everyone else.

So are we really the same as everyone else? Is our final destination the only difference? Or is there something fundamentally distinct about the core of our being that sets us apart from everyone else? Until we answer these questions, we're left to wallow in confusion about a fundamental issue: Who am I?

BORN SLAVES

As a devout Jew, Saul of Tarsus wanted to keep the law and do right. His intentions were in line with what God had commanded. But he didn't end up carrying out those intentions. Lost or saved, most of us can identify with the frustration of life under law.

Paul goes out of his way to clarify that the problem was *not* his intentions. Read carefully, and you'll find that the problem was something else:

> For I know that nothing good dwells in me, that is, in my flesh; for the willing is present in me, but the doing of the good is not. For the good that I want, I do not do, but I practice the very evil that I do not want.
>
> ROMANS 7:18–19 NASB

So why was Saul of Tarsus not able to do good things? In the next verse, he reveals the cause of his puzzling behavior: "Now if I do what I do not want to do, *it is no longer I who do it*, but *it is sin living in me that does it*" (Romans 7:20, italics added).

Without a doubt, he's passing off credit to *something other than himself*. If you haven't caught this important truth yet, take a few minutes to read the second half of Romans 7 slowly. Notice what he emphasizes twice, both in verse 17 and in verse 20.

Theologians debate whether or not Paul was saved when he went through the Romans 7 experience. I think Romans 7 recounts his struggle as a Jew, since he announces himself to be "in the flesh" (verse 5 NASB) and "sold as a slave to sin" (verse 14). To me, this sounds like lost talk. Once saved, the apostle Paul knew that he had died and was freed from sin.

Whether Romans 7 is describing a pre-salvation or a post-salvation experience is not crucial. Regardless of one's view on this issue, the point is that there's a sin principle within the physical body.* And this sin principle is aroused when we, whether saved or lost, try to live up to the law or any lawlike standard.

> There's a sin principle within the physical body.

Neither our bodies nor our connection to the physical changed at salvation. So once we're saved, sin is *still* present in our bodies. As we'll discuss later, we're now dead to sin and can therefore resist its prodding. But sin itself isn't dead. As our experience tells us, it's very much alive.

Sin is *in us*, but it's *not us*.

---

*See Sidelight 6 on p. 233.

The Devil Made Me Do It?

Does this mean we can shirk responsibility for our actions? Should we conclude that when we sin, the Devil made us do it, and so it's not our fault?

We know from Romans 6 that it's *our* responsibility to not let sin run our lives. Paul admonishes us to resist this rogue force and not allow it to take control. Clearly, there's a choice. We're urged to recognize the presence of sin and say no to it: "Do not let *sin* reign in your mortal body so that you obey *its* evil desires" (Romans 6:12, italics added).

Notice to whom the evil desires belong, namely, to sin. If we give in to sin, we're buying the lie that we *want* to sin. Yes, we're not yielding to God. But we're also not yielding to our own selves. Instead, we're giving in to thoughts that didn't originate with us. They're coming from a sinister source, and for that reason they will never fulfill.

We can allow sin to have its way with us, but what benefit will we really get? Sure, there may be a temporal and fleeting sense of fulfillment but only at a base (fleshly) level. In the believer, this feeling will eventually give way to remorse and a sense of our higher calling.

The reason for this sense of higher calling is twofold: the presence of Christ within and the believer's new human spirit that's joined with him. As heavenly people, we despise the flesh and the power of sin. The core of our being cries out to fulfill the destiny set before us.

A Parasite

Imagine that you are going to a tropical climate for a vacation. After you check into the hotel, you throw on your sandals and head down the trail toward the beach. Along the way, however, a local parasite attaches itself to your foot. Over time, it burrows further and further in until it's lodged deep inside your foot—so deep you don't realize it's there.

Over the next few months, the parasite begins to grow, feeding off of your life. Eventually, its ravages begin to send pain messages to your brain. As time goes on, the pain becomes increasingly difficult to bear. You begin thinking, "There's something seriously wrong with me. There's something wrong with my foot." Not knowing about what lies *within* your foot, you assume the problem is your foot itself.

In the months and years that follow, you consult with numerous doctors, but no one detects the presence of the parasite. Eventually, you conclude there's only one solution—amputation. You must rid yourself of the source of the problem. To do so, you reason you'll need to sever a part of yourself.

What a tragedy! If only someone could detect the parasite, you'd know the truth.

Although not actually physical, the power of sin is much like a parasite that has found its way inside your body. This parasite lies within us, but it's not us. When our mind receives messages from the power of sin, these messages can feel or sound just like us—especially if we're not aware that our old self is dead and gone and that we truly *don't want* to sin. If we're not aware of who we really are, sin can make us think that its messages originate with us. After a sinful thought passes through our minds, sin can even turn right around and hit us with an accusatory thought: "How could I, a Christian, even *think* something like that?"

Have you ever found yourself surprised at your own thinking? Do you ever wonder how you could be so sincere about your life in Christ and yet think such things? It's not because we are half dirty and half clean. It's because there's a battle going on within us. And understanding the nature of that battle is crucial if we desire any real change in the outcome.

18

IT'S EASY TO SEE WHY WE OFTEN ASSUME THAT THE OLD SELF IS only positionally dead or is slowly dying off. The old self must still be around, because we're still getting these nagging sinful thoughts. Right?

But it seems the Scriptures leave no room for misunderstanding concerning the issue of the old self. If you're in Christ, your old self is nowhere to be found within you. The old self is dead, buried, and gone. However, we now understand why believers still sin. We sin because of the continued presence of something called the power of sin—"hooking" us in various ways through the flesh.

I've read countless books on theology and Christian living that start with the premise that we still sin, and then they conclude that the old self is still around.* They decide that Christians have two selves and still need to "die to self." And sometimes I've had people point to these verses in Ephesians to support a dying-to-self theology:

> That, however, is not the way of life [giving yourselves over to sensuality] you learned when you heard about Christ and were taught in him in accordance with the truth that is in Jesus. You were taught, with regard to

---

*See Sidelight 7 on pp. 233–34.

your former way of life, to put off your old self, which is
being corrupted by its deceitful desires; to be made new
in the attitude of your minds.

EPHESIANS 4:20–23

But apparently this passage is addressing behavior (way of life),
and Paul is simply pointing out that they were originally taught
that life in Christ brings behavior change.

The phrase *die to self* is nowhere to be found, and the phrase *put
off your old self* is a bit ambiguous. Is it a present-tense command
for them to obey right now? Or is it what they were taught (past
tense) when Paul first instructed them? Most likely it is the latter,
given that Colossians clearly states that Christians have taken off
(past tense) our old self at salvation:

Do not lie to each other, since you *have taken off* your old
self with its practices and *have put on* the new self, which is
being renewed in knowledge in the image of its Creator.

COLOSSIANS 3:9–10, italics added

Instead of trying to somehow "die to self," which seems to me
to be equivalent to exploring a bottomless pit,* I think we should
start with the premise found in Scripture that the old self is dead
and gone. We should then conclude that there must be some *other*
reason why we still sin. As we take this approach, Paul's teachings
on the flesh and the power of sin within us make a lot of sense.

Is this an important distinction? Absolutely. I would argue that
it's essential for both a proper self-image and daily victory over
temptation. We must realize that saying no to sin is not saying
no to ourselves. As God's workmanship, our regenerated selves
are not the problem. Sin is the problem, and our calling as new
creations in Christ is to say no to sin and say yes to who we truly
are.

---

*See Sidelight 8 on pp. 234–35.

In the Body?

As you read the passage below, take note of the two actors—
Saul the Pharisee and "another law." Here the phrase *another law*
means a different principle, force, or power. Notice where this
rogue agent is located:

> So I find this law at work: When I want to do good, evil
> is right there *with me*. For in my inner being I delight in
> God's law; but I see another law at work *in the members*
> *of my body*, waging war against the law of my mind and
> making me a prisoner of the law of sin at work *within*
> *my members*.
>
> ROMANS 7:21–23 NIV, italics added

There's a battle within our very own bodies. The key to winning
a battle is to understand who is fighting against whom and what
strategies are being employed. Imagine the confusion if, in the midst
of a battle, you mistakenly begin to fight against your own army!

From Saul to Paul

Saul of Tarsus hated being overtaken by the rebel force called sin.
He cried out for freedom from it. And he eventually found that
freedom through undergoing a radical surgery:

> Wretched man that I am! Who will set me free from
> the body of this death? Thanks be to God through Jesus
> Christ our Lord! So then, on the one hand *I myself with*
> *my mind* am serving the law of God, but on the other,
> with my flesh the law of sin.
>
> ROMANS 7:24–25 NASB, italics added

The Pharisee was frustrated with his spiritual experience. He
cognitively understood what the law mandated, but he had no

power to carry it out. The power of sin got the best of him every time. But through his spiritual co-crucifixion with Christ, Saul became Paul. Under the New, Paul found victory over the power of sin that had overwhelmed him for so long.

As Christians, we have gone through the same surgery. We're now on God's team, and we want what he wants. Our fight is *not* against ourselves. The battle is against a parasitic force within us. That force may appear to be us. It may sound like us within our thought life. It may even feel like us within our emotions. Nevertheless, God has exposed the Deceiver's lie. It is most certainly *not* us.

> Our fight is *not* against ourselves.

We are new creations with God's desires stamped on our hearts and minds. What a truth to relish! What a truth to set us free!

WHAT'S THE BIG DEAL?

It's liberating to realize that the power of sin is the source of temptation, not our own self.* However, does this knowledge alone really help bring about a marked improvement in our responses to temptation? Well, it certainly can't hurt! But there are a few more pieces of the puzzle to put in place. It's not enough to know the source of the temptation. It's also important to realize that we have *the power to resist* that source.

Nonbelievers are spiritually harnessed to the power of sin. As a horse is led by reins, nonbelievers are controlled by the reign of sin. When a person comes to Christ, their old self, which was controlled by sin, dies through the work of the cross. A new self is raised through resurrection in Christ. If we're in Christ, we don't have to submit to sin any longer. We're free to choose expressions of life instead of always expressing sin and death:

---

*See Sidelight 9 on p. 235.

> We know that our old self was crucified with [Christ]
> so that the body ruled by sin might be done away with
> [made powerless], that we should no longer be slaves
> to sin—because anyone who has died has been set free
> from sin.
>
> ROMANS 6:6–7

Paul goes on to urge us to count ourselves dead to sin but alive to God (Romans 6:11). Some English translations use the term *reckon* here: "reckon yourselves to be dead indeed to sin" (NKJV). Whether one prefers *reckon* or *count* or *consider*, it makes little difference as long as we realize that our reckoning is not what causes this to become reality. Instead of our "making it a reality," we're invited to bank on the fact that our death to sin is already real.

Some would put the burden on Christians to believe hard enough in order to make our death to sin a reality. This isn't the meaning of *reckon, count,* or *consider.* These words mean "to rely on the fact" that you're dead to sin because God has already said it is so (and it *is* so!): "In the same way, count yourselves dead to sin but alive to God in Christ Jesus" (Romans 6:11).

Here we're invited to live in reality. If we're living under the assumption that sin is the most natural thing for us, then we're being deluded. We're different from the way we were before. We're now alive to God, and we must come to grips with an essential truth: *It is more normal, more fitting, and more like us to display the fruit of the Spirit than it is for us to display sin!*

NEGATIVE TO POSITIVE

Whenever I read Romans 6, it makes me think of a numeric scale ranging from negative ten to positive ten. Negative ten would represent "alive to sin," while positive ten would represent "alive to God." It's not enough for us to be dead to sin. That would merely cause us to register as a zero or neutral on the scale. Instead, God has taken us all the way from a negative ten (alive to sin) to a positive ten for his use. He not only made us dead to sin; he made us alive to himself. Likewise, he not only removed our unrighteousness; he then made us righteous.

> You are now 100 percent OK with God.

God is communicating that you are now 100 percent OK with him. God doesn't spiritually join himself to neutral people. He has reserved himself exclusively for perfect, righteous saints.

The amazing news is that he has made us precisely that!

My intent is to put the pieces together to explain why a perfectly righteous new creation still struggles with sin in order to show that the person we used to be in Adam has indeed been obliterated. I don't believe this should be relegated to the realm of the positional, the symbolic, or the "true in heaven only" category. To do so results in double-talk that is inconsistent with the "old self" passages and in my experience fails to provide believers with any real answers for daily living.

The solution is to consult the same author who spoke of the old self's crucifixion to see if there's an explanation for our continued struggle. Paul comes through by attributing our current battle to the ongoing presence of two forces—the flesh and the power of sin. Neither of these is the old self.

God calls us to consider his explanation of our ongoing struggle as truth. Why? Because if we don't, we're living under the delusion that we're no different from the guy next door.

And that's a pitiful, half-baked gospel.

GO OUT ON A LIMB!

Many of us have already gone to extremes in our faith. We believe that God spoke the universe into existence. We believe that a flood engulfed the earth and that a man spent three days in a big fish. To top it off, we believe that Jesus rose from the dead and then floated up into the sky amidst many onlookers.

What crazy events we've chosen to swallow as truth! Is the death of our old self any more difficult to believe? Alongside an explanation for why we still sin, I think it's much easier. So why not *reinterpret* our thought life in light of this revelation concerning the flesh and the power of sin?

The miracle of spiritual regeneration is a concept that has existed for thousands of years. Even Old Testament prophets spoke of the miracles that would one day take place within the children of God under the New:

> I will give you *a new heart* and put *a new spirit* in you; I will remove from you your heart of stone and give you a heart of flesh. And I will put *my Spirit* in you and move you to follow my decrees and be careful to keep my laws.
>
> EZEKIEL 36:26–27, italics added

God gives us a new heart. This means that our core desires are now changed. We also receive a new spirit. Notice that the word *spirit* here is translated with a lowercase *s* to communicate that it is our human spirit that is exchanged. Finally, we also receive God's Spirit within us. Although many Christians are aware that the Holy Spirit is within them, we may not differentiate him from our human spirit that has died and been re-created to be like Christ.

> It is our human spirit that is exchanged.

The Scriptures speak clearly about our union with Christ. It's essential to understand not only the presence of Christ in us but also *who we are* in him. I hope this brief look into our real identity has sparked your desire to examine further who you are, what type of heart you have, and what it means to be one spirit with God (1 Corinthians 6:17).

We're invited to celebrate a radical truth—a truth that has been misunderstood over the centuries due to our inability to explain ongoing sinning or our fear that others will think we're claiming sinless perfection in our performance. Once we accept God's explanation for continued sinning, we're rejuvenated to consider our spiritual death and resurrection as an actual fact that will forever change the way we approach life: "Therefore, if anyone is in Christ, the new creation has come: The old has gone, the new is here!" (2 Corinthians 5:17).

PART 5

cheating on Jesus

Let us remember that [God] is holy and he is righteous,
and that a holy and righteous God has the right to say that
the blood is acceptable in his eyes and has fully satisfied him.

Watchman Nee (1903 – 1972)

19

PICTURE THE SCENE. AN ISRAELITE CAMP IN THE DESERT, SEVERAL thousand years ago. The tabernacle, pitched on top of a hill in the center of the camp. The high priest, running down the hillside shouting that he has found the perfect spotless lamb, which will be sacrificed on behalf of all the people, taking care of their sins for the rest of their lives.

Imagine the excitement! After that one final sacrifice, all the men of Israel gather to begin tearing down the tabernacle. Then they move on with a whole new way of life. No longer do they have to worry about sacrifices to clean up their track record. Instead, they can live guilt free, knowing that a perfect lamb has done away with their sins once and for all.

Of course, this never happened. Instead, what we see is the Israelites having to offer animal sacrifices over and over throughout their history, because no single sacrifice was sufficient to perfectly cleanse them. Hebrews explains clearly:

> [The law] can never, by the same sacrifices repeated endlessly year after year, make perfect those who draw near to worship. Otherwise, would they not have stopped being offered? For the worshipers *would have been cleansed once for all*, and would no longer have felt guilty for their sins.
>
> HEBREWS 10:1–2, italics added

Although we never read of an Old Testament priest finding the perfect lamb, this announcement was, in fact, made. When? Not long before the sacrifice that would initiate the New. Upon seeing Jesus, John the Baptist declared, "Look, the Lamb of God, who takes away the sin of the world!" (John 1:29).

Today, we have a perfect Lamb in the person of Jesus Christ. His sacrifice rendered the temple ceremonies null and void. There's no longer any purpose for the tabernacle, the temple, or the daily sacrifices.

Because Jesus Christ's sacrifice cleansed us *once for all*, not repeatedly over time, there's no method or procedure required for us to remain forgiven. We're invited to depend on the onetime sacrifice as the means to lifelong forgiveness, without any strings attached: "Christ died for sins *once for all*, the righteous for the unrighteous, to bring you to God" (1 Peter 3:18 NIV, italics added).

> There's no method or procedure required for us to remain forgiven.

INTERVIEW WITH A JEW

The issue concerning forgiveness becomes crystal clear if we understand God's economy, which hasn't changed since the beginning of time. To illustrate, let's travel back in time as an investigative reporter to interview a Jew as he exits the tabernacle.

"Excuse me, Mr. Jew, you seem very relieved compared with the way you looked when you entered the tabernacle just a short time ago. What's your secret? What makes you feel so much better about the past year of sinning? Did you promise Yahweh that you'd do better this coming year—that you would turn over a new leaf?"

The Jewish man responds, "No, nothing like that took place."

Slightly confused, you press on to discover the truth. "Well, did you carefully name off each sin and ask Yahweh to cover your sins?"

"Certainly not!" the Jewish man exclaims.

"Well, then, what *exactly* made you feel relief from guilt for all the sins you've committed over the past twelve months?"

At this point, any well-educated Jew would give the same response: "What made me feel better? The blood of bulls and goats that covered my past sins, of course! Yahweh has always demanded a *blood* sacrifice for sins, and now—because of the animal I bought to offer as a sacrifice—my sins are covered!"

This is God's economy. It has always been the case that one thing brings forgiveness of sins, namely, blood—nothing else: "Without the shedding of blood there is no forgiveness" (Hebrews 9:22).

NOTHING BUT THE BLOOD

If we accept God's blood-only economy, it revolutionizes our perspective on how we stand before him. The bottom line is that no amount of dialoguing with God about our sins will bring us more forgiveness. No amount of asking God to forgive us will initiate his cleansing in our lives. Instead, blood sacrifice is the only action that results in forgiveness and cleansing. This was true in the Old Testament, and there's no exception today.

> No amount of dialoguing with God about our sins will bring us *more* forgiveness.

Because there are no more blood sacrifices being made for sins, we must conclude something about the onetime sacrifice of Jesus Christ: either it was or was not sufficient to bring a lifetime of forgiveness and cleansing. If so, then God is satisfied regarding our sins, both now and in eternity. If not, then we are stuck with no biblical way of dealing with God's wrath toward us.

Unfortunately, right here is where I see many of us getting

creative, as we use terms such as *positional truth* and *heavenly book-keeping*. We say we're forgiven and cleansed "in God's eyes." But then we claim that Christ's death does *not* translate into "once for all" forgiveness in the here and now. Perhaps it just feels too easy: "You mean I don't have to do anything? That doesn't sound right." Our human pride won't allow us to enjoy *that* kind of grace.

Some exhort believers to do something, such as asking for forgiveness, to impel God so that he will *actually* forgive and cleanse them. This certainly satisfies us; there's nothing like a daily list of sins to pore over to relieve us from guilt.

Some claim a procedure is necessary to "appropriate" or "activate" forgiveness. They say we must "keep short accounts" of our sins and ask God to forgive and cleanse us in order to "make it real in our own experience." But didn't God announce that only one thing—blood—brings forgiveness and cleansing?

Without realizing it, we end up believing that Christ's blood has real effects only for heaven. If we want to maintain a cleansed state before God here on earth, we begin to think it comes through a work that *we* initiate through remembering, confessing, asking, and claiming. Ultimately, it becomes *our* responsibility to make the cross carry real benefits in the present.

In adopting this fine-sounding belief system, we fail to recognize that the cross is a historical event. Its effects are already accomplished, no matter what we believe or claim.

We don't initiate forgiveness, because we cannot. Only blood brings forgiveness. Our acts of remembrance, confession, asking forgiveness, and claiming—whether done with good intentions or not—don't cause more blood to be shed.

I'll discuss the scriptural idea of "confession" in a moment, but realistically, we only have two choices: (1) accept as fact the complete, unconditional forgiveness that God purchased through the crushing of his Son, or (2) create some system of our own to feel better about our sins.

Jews actually felt better (yes, in the real world!) because of the blood of bulls and goats that was shed on their behalf. There was no further "activation" needed to appro-priate that forgiveness. The act of the high priest's slaughtering the animal was suffi-cient to cause the entire nation of Israel to shout from the rooftops with real-world relief from guilt. The only difference between then and now was that sacrifices of Old were continuous, whereas Jesus' sacrifice was once for all.

> Only blood brings forgiveness.

What then are we saying about the sacrifice of Jesus when we insist that something further be done to "activate" it? In essence, we're insulting the work of Calvary. We're valuing the Son's sac-rifice even less than the people of the Old valued their animal sacrifices.

20

PICTURE MY SON GAVIN'S FIRST BIRTHDAY PARTY. FRIENDS AND family gather in our backyard, and on the patio table sit dozens of birthday gifts and a big chocolate cake.

To kick the event off with a bang, I feel I should start with a speech. I hold Gavin high atop my shoulders and begin to share what a joy he is to me and his mother. I tell cute and funny stories about things he has done, how he is growing so fast, and all the things we have to look forward to with him.

While I am sharing about Gavin, a friend at the back of the crowd shouts, "I've got a drinking problem." On the heels of that comment, someone else mutters, "I've got a critical spirit." Yet another confesses, "I struggle with lust."

Soon chatter gives way to more chatter, and the whole focus of the event shifts. No longer is anyone concerned with Gavin and what I have to say about him. Instead, everyone seems to be consumed with their own issues.

How ridiculous! How inappropriate! Of course, this event never really occurred. But I tell the tale to illustrate a point. God has lifted his Son high, seating him at his right hand. God has declared that his Son's works are awesome and that we should marvel at them. The central purpose of our lives is to focus on the Son. In so doing, we please the Father.

Just as I hoped that all would genuinely celebrate Gavin's birthday, God the Father wants us to be obsessed with his begotten. We are to eat of his flesh, drink of his blood, and relish his finished work on the cross.

Sadly, often we get so self-consumed that it's nearly impossible to get Christians to talk about anything other than our sins. It's as if our sense of importance stems from the fact that we're dealing with struggles. These struggles enable us to think about ourselves, converse about ourselves, and even obsess about ourselves—with a spiritual label on it all.

We can become so focused on our struggles that we can't believe God wants us to look elsewhere. We become convinced that our sins are different—that somehow God hasn't forgotten them and asked us to move on. As we wallow in our failures, we miss the privilege of celebrating. We miss the reason for the party.

If the ridiculous circumstances at Gavin's party were actually to occur, my only response to those who interrupted would be, "Join the club! We all struggle. But we're not here to focus on your issues. We're here to focus on my son." Similarly, we're invited to fix our eyes on Jesus, since he is worthy of celebration.

Are you consumed with your sins when God says he remembers them no more? Are you willing to agree that the focus is no longer on your failures? Will you please the Father through obsession with the Son?

The Son of God has finished his work. He is risen and is now seated in heavenly places. There's only one appropriate response. All eyes on him!

No Repeat Needed

Today I don't see us making it a big deal that Christ died *only once*. It seems to be a rather insignificant point. But to the Jewish mindset, it was extremely important. Hebrews goes to great lengths to emphasize that Christ died only once and that he's not in heaven dying over and over. We might say, "Of course, he's not up there dying all the time!" So why even mention it? Why make such a big deal about it? Well, let's first take a look at how the author of Hebrews puts it:

> Nor did he enter heaven to offer himself *again and again*, the way the high priest enters the Most Holy Place every year with blood that is not his own. Otherwise Christ would have had to suffer many times since the creation of the world. But he has appeared *once for all* at the culmination of the ages to do away with sin by the sacrifice of himself.
>
> HEBREWS 9:25–26, italics added

> Unlike the other high priests, [Christ] does not need to offer sacrifices *day after day*, first for his own sins, and then for the sins of the people. He sacrificed for their sins *once for all* when he offered himself.
>
> HEBREWS 7:27, italics added

Why emphasize how many times Jesus died? A devout Jew could connect the dots quickly. The thought process might look like this:

- Only blood brings forgiveness.
- Jesus' blood will never be shed again.
- Therefore God is satisfied.
- And I enjoy lifelong and eternal cleansing.

We need to grasp how central the cross was to Jews. The impact on their lives was dramatic. Accepting Jesus' sacrifice on the cross meant that all of their law-centered attempts to motivate

God to forgive them came to a screeching halt. Temple sacrifices no longer made any sense.

The writer of Hebrews pleads with his fellow Jews to abandon the dead works of the temple. He begs them to hang on to Jesus plus *nothing*. How insulting it would be to God if any Jewish believer were to return to participation in the temple sacrifices! They would be publicly disgracing Jesus Christ, since they sought another means of forgiveness after being introduced to the cross. Their attitude would be something like this: "I believe that Jesus died for my sins, but just in case I'll continue to participate in animal sacrifices." And some actually *encouraged* this double-mindedness in the early church!

What about us today? How does our doubt about the once-for-all sacrifice manifest itself? We don't express our doubt through temple ceremonies or through animal sacrifices in our backyards. We employ more subtle means of insulting God. Rather than publicly disgracing him, we *privately* disgrace him in our mind-sets and belief systems.

> We employ more subtle means of insulting God.

If the writer of Hebrews were to address us today, he'd challenge our double-mindedness as we perform theological gymnastics to make ourselves feel cleansed before God. He'd confront us when we invent nonbiblical terminology and propose that we're forgiven from God's vantage point but not *actually* forgiven without a "method." He'd accuse us of doing exactly what the recipients of his letter were doing—insulting the Spirit of grace.

MORE THAN ATONEMENT

It's fair to make some comparison between the Old and the New. Under both systems, only blood brought forgiveness. But there's a significant difference between blood sacrifices under the Old and the one sacrifice initiating the New. As we begin to look at the difference, let's return to John the Baptist's announcement concerning Jesus as sacrifice: "Look, the Lamb of God, who takes away the sin of the world!" (John 1:29).

While old sacrifices brought atonement (covering) of sins, the blood of Jesus accomplished something greater. The blood of Jesus *took away* our sins! Animal blood couldn't achieve this. There was never an animal sacrifice qualified to do so. Hebrews brings this truth to our attention to highlight just how significant the cross is. The cross wholly and unquestionably dealt with our sins forever.

> The cross wholly and unquestionably dealt with our sins forever.

Although Old Testament sacrifices were mandated by God for the nation of Israel, they paled in comparison to Jesus' work on the cross. Old Testament believers who offered blood sacrifices found themselves yearning for the Lamb to come: "Those sacrifices are an annual reminder of sins. It is impossible for the blood of bulls and goats to take away sins" (Hebrews 10:3–4).

On some level, they were aware that sacrifices under the Old were only a shadow of things to come. Sure, they experienced the benefit of having their sins temporarily covered. But it would only be through the blood of Jesus that their sin problem would truly be solved. They were staking a claim on an IOU or promissory note from God that was cashed in at the cross. This is why John the Baptist was so excited as he announced the appearance of the One who would *take away* (not just cover) the sin of the world.

FORGIVEN BUT FEARFUL?

Jesus Christ so thoroughly obliterated our deserved punishment for sins that God will never refer to our sins again. We nod our heads in agreement that Jesus died for our sins and took them away, but soon afterward we find ourselves buying the idea that we'll be judged for our sins when Jesus returns. How could we be judged for our sins if he has taken them away? How could we be punished for our sins when he remembers them no longer? And the only worthy punishment for sins is death, and death is precisely what Jesus experienced on our behalf.

Read carefully the words of these two Jewish writers who express excitement about the perfect Lamb and the *effects* of his sacrifice:

> Christ also, having been offered once to bear the sins of many, will appear a second time for salvation *without reference to sin*, to those who eagerly await Him.
>
> HEBREWS 9:28 NASB, italics added

> He is the one who *turns aside God's wrath*, taking away our sins, and not only ours, but also the sins of the whole world.
>
> 1 JOHN 2:2 (see NIV text note), italics added

If we miss the message of the gospel, it holds no power to alter natural mind-sets that control us. Partial forgiveness provides partial relief from guilt but breeds an unhealthy fear of judgment. Real forgiveness means that the sin issue is *over*. Real forgiveness means that there's no present or future punishment for sins. Jesus' death satisfied God forever. And there's nothing about us that will ever anger him again: "When he had received the drink, Jesus said, 'It is finished.' With that, he bowed his head and gave up his spirit" (John 19:30).

> We find ourselves buying the idea that we'll be judged for our sins.

21

A CHAIR WAS A FORBIDDEN PIECE OF FURNITURE INSIDE THE JEWISH tabernacle and later in the temple. Why? Imagine for a moment that you're an average citizen of Israel. You enter the temple on the Day of Atonement and are greeted by a priest lounging in a La-Z-Boy. What would this communicate to you? He must have nothing left to do! To avoid this false impression, God didn't allow such a scene to take place. He forbade Levitical priests to sit down on the job, so that the image of *unfinished* business would be imprinted on their consciences.

Hebrews contrasts the constant standing and ongoing religious performances of Old priests with our *seated* High Priest, who will never again offer another sacrifice for sins:

> Day after day *every priest stands* and performs his religious duties; again and again he offers the same sacrifices, which can never take away sins. But when this priest [Jesus] had offered for all time one sacrifice for sins, *he sat down* at the right hand of God.
>
> HEBREWS 10:11 – 12, italics added

> After [Jesus] had provided purification for sins, he sat down at the right hand of the Majesty in heaven.
>
> HEBREWS 1:3

Grasping this truth can revolutionize our understanding of how pure and clean we are before God. We're invited to recognize our High Priest as seated at the right hand of the Father, with nothing left to do about our sins. The work is completed, and we're now forgiven for all time.

We're now forgiven for all time.

Our past, present, and future sins were dealt with simultaneously through the cross. God didn't discriminate with regard to time of occurrence. All of our sins were in the future when Jesus died. He looked down the entire timeline of human existence and took away all sins. Whether the sins occurred two thousand years before or after the cross made no difference. When Jesus finished wiping out all record of our sins, he took a seat. And he has been relaxing at God's right hand ever since.

What position are you in with regard to your sins? Are you standing up, running around, and trying to make up for them? Attempting to get forgiven, to get cleansed? Or are you seated with Jesus Christ in a relaxed position? Do you realize that your Savior has taken them away once and for all?

Christians today talk about wanting to be like Jesus and to think like Jesus. We often hear the popular question, "What would Jesus do?" Thinking like Jesus involves having the same attitude about our sins that he does. He assures us that the sin issue is over. There's no other act that will make us more forgiven than we already are: *"By one offering [Jesus] has perfected for all time those who are sanctified"* (Hebrews 10:14 NASB, italics added).

Are you willing to be like Jesus by forgetting your sins? Are you eager to agree with God that you're a forgiven person? Would you go so far as to agree with the writer of Hebrews that you've been made perfect forever? Anything short of these astounding claims is not faith in the gospel. God wants us to know that *real* forgiveness has been accomplished on our behalf. It's ours to enjoy. Freedom from guilt is our daily destiny as believers in Jesus.

IT'S ALL IN THE PAST

Nothing is more convincing than the numerous Bible passages that refer to our forgiveness as a completed act. When it comes to forgiveness, most of these passages talk about it using the past tense:

> When you were dead in your sins ..., God made you alive with Christ. He forgave us all our sins, having canceled the written code, with its regulations, that was against us and that stood opposed to us; he took it away, nailing it to the cross.
>
> COLOSSIANS 2:13–14 NIV

> Be kind and compassionate to one another, forgiving each other, just as in Christ God forgave you.
>
> EPHESIANS 4:32

> "Their sins and lawless acts
> I will remember no more."
>
> And where these have been forgiven, sacrifice for sin is no longer necessary.
>
> HEBREWS 10:17–18

Whether it's expressed as "forgave" or "have been forgiven" makes little difference. The concept is plain and obvious. Jesus shed his blood, and this brought forgiveness. Since he doesn't die daily, our forgiveness is not issued daily. Since he'll never die again, there's no further forgiveness needed. We have been forgiven, and therefore we live in a forgiven state.

> Since Jesus doesn't die daily, our forgiveness is not issued daily.

PERPETUAL PROPOSALS

Let's say you are a married man. Imagine if every night before you went to sleep, you leaned over to your wife and asked her to marry you. It's just something that would make you feel better—asking her again and again. It's your way of confirming that you're married. So every night you say, "Honey, will you marry me?" The words you choose are no big deal. It's just semantics. You know you're really married, but you just like to ask her over and over.

This ritual is more than a bit strange, isn't it? Your wife would never let you get away with something so ridiculous. Semantics? Hardly. Repeating a question like that over and over might even be a little insulting.

If I were to try this with my wife, she would ask me to reconsider my thought processes: "Don't you remember the ceremony? The vows? The witnesses? We were married years ago. I have the photo album right here. It's now a past event. We live in a constant state of being married. There's no need to ask me over and over if I'll marry you."

It's the same way with our forgiven state. And it's not just semantics. It matters. Have you thought about how many times the epistles urge us to ask God for forgiveness? The answer is *zero* times. You won't find a single epistle that suggests that we ask God for forgiveness. Why not? Because the writers penned their words *after* the death of Jesus. They were fully aware of their forgiveness as an accomplished fact.

Like my wife's recollection of our wedding, the writers remembered the "ceremony" of the cross and the "vow" made by God to remember their sins no more. In fact, some of them were eyewitnesses of the once-for-all sacrifice. It wouldn't make sense to urge their readers to ask God for forgiveness.

These authors were Jews by birth. They were fully aware of God's economy—only blood brings forgiveness. In their minds, asking for forgiveness would be equivalent to requesting that Jesus hang on a cross over and over again. You know—one death for today's sins, another death for tomorrow's sins, and so forth.

They knew better.

22

But what about 1 John 1:9 — "*If we confess our sins, [God] is faithful and just and will forgive us our sins and purify us from all unrighteousness*"? (italics added).

At first glance, this well-known verse appears to muddy the waters concerning once-for-all forgiveness. In many books and articles on the topic of forgiveness, this verse often serves as the foundation on which the author's belief system is constructed.

Theologians and Christian authors will often agree with John that "your sins have been forgiven on account of [Jesus'] name" (1 John 2:12). But later you find them essentially saying that confession is needed to *cause* God to forgive you. The problem is that both statements can't be true at the same time. Either we've been forgiven, or there's a condition for us to be forgiven.

> Either we've been forgiven, or there's a condition for us to be forgiven.

To resolve this dilemma, some have proposed the following: Christians are forgiven eternally in God's heavenly record books. However, unless Christians keep short accounts with God through daily confession of sins, they can't experience God's cleansing during life on earth. Hence, they claim that 1 John 1:9 is the believer's "bar of soap" to maintain daily fellowship with God.

And they use terms such as *judicial, patriarchal,* and *forensic* as they delicately dance around the reality of once-for-all forgiveness and push the idea of a two-tiered forgiveness system in which eternally God is satisfied, but right now we somehow maintain our own daily cleansing through a confession ritual.

I frequently come across this line of thinking in which 1 John 1:9 is the one and only hallmark verse. But we know we shouldn't develop theologies based principally around one verse. It's important to recognize that this verse stands as the only one of its kind. No other verse in the epistles appears to place a conditional "if" on forgiveness and cleansing.

> No other verse in the epistles appears to place a conditional "if" on forgiveness and cleansing.

So if there was a method for maintaining daily cleansing, the Romans were apparently unaware of it. If there was a prescription for keeping short accounts with God, the Galatians seemed to have had no exposure to it. If there was a need to ask God for forgiveness, the Ephesians were apparently not privy to it. Similarly, the Corinthians, Philippians, Colossians, and Thessalonians also seemed to have missed this teaching.

If there were a daily method to maintain good status (fellowship) with God through ongoing confession of sins or pleas for forgiveness, wouldn't you think it'd be mentioned in at least one epistle? Did God accidentally leave it out? Certainly not!

So let's take a closer look at 1 John 1:9 to understand John's intended audience and the context of this peculiar verse.

ADDRESSING HERESIES

From the beginning of John's first chapter, we see him addressing prominent heresies in the early church. John begins his letter with words such as *heard, seen, looked at,* and *touched* to describe his interactions with Jesus. He does this to emphasize the physicality of Jesus.

Today, we take for granted that Jesus was physical. Of course he was! No argument there. But two millennia ago early forms of Gnostic thought infiltrated the church and popularized the idea that Jesus was only spirit. Early Gnostics claimed that God would never stoop so low as to take on human flesh. So the apostle John purposely uses physical words in his opening statement to challenge this Gnostic heresy. Later, he says that anyone who doesn't believe that Jesus came in human flesh is *not from God* (1 John 4:3).

If that's the case, then who was John's audience in his first chapter? True believers don't claim that Jesus lacked a physical body. So John is *not* correcting believers in his opening statement. He's addressing Gnostics who had infiltrated the early church and were teaching false doctrines. After establishing the physicality of Jesus, John then writes, *"If we claim to be without sin*, we deceive ourselves and the truth is not in us" (1 John 1:8, italics added).

Why is John now concerned about those who claim they're sinless? Do you know any true believers today who say they've never sinned? Of course not! What do you have to do to become a believer in Christ? Admit you're a sinner! Someone who claims they have never sinned is *not* a Christian. So here John is concerned for *un*believers.

Interestingly, early Gnostic philosophers didn't just deny the physicality of Jesus; *they also denied the reality of sin.* Gnostics claimed that sin wasn't real or didn't matter, since it took place in the physical world. So John opens his letter by attacking two Gnostic heresies: (1) Jesus as nonphysical, and (2) sin as a nonreality.

Understanding John's purpose in opening his letter this way is crucial. A poor interpretation of verse 9 leads many Christians astray. Again, verse 9 declares, "If we confess our sins, [God] is faithful and just and will forgive us our sins and purify us from all unrighteousness."

Some claim that this verse must refer to Christians, since John uses the word *we*. If that were true, one should hold that all preceding and following verses using *we* also refer to Christians. But this isn't the case.

John uses *we* to politely combat Gnostic heresy. We see this technique in the following:

- If *we* claim to be without sin . . . (1 John 1:8)
- If *we* claim we have not sinned . . . (1 John 1:10)

Similarly, John uses the word *us* to draw conclusions such as these:

- the truth is not in *us* (1 John 1:8)
- [God's] word is not in *us* (1 John 1:10 NASB)

Is John referring to believers here? When referring to people who don't have the truth in them or God's word in them, does he include himself and the church in that group? Certainly not! John is politely saying that if we *humans* claim we have no sin, we're liars and don't have Christ (the Word and the Truth) in us. Clearly, John is talking about *un*believers.

So if an unbeliever has bought into the heresy of sinless perfection, what's the only sensible solution? Let's reread verse 9 to see if we can get John's intent: "If we confess our sins, [God] is faithful and just and will forgive us our sins and purify us from all unrighteousness."

> 1 John 1:9 is an invitation to become a Christian.

Verse 9 is a remedy for unbelievers who have been influenced by Gnostic peer pressure and are now claiming sinless perfection. John is essentially asking, "Instead of claiming that you have no sin, will you consider changing your mind? Instead of claiming you've never sinned, how about agreeing with God?" He's inviting Gnostics to rethink their point of view. If they'll admit their sinfulness, then God can do a saving work in their lives.

So 1 John 1:9 is an invitation to become a Christian. And it certainly holds relevance today. If anyone claims to be without sin, they're wrong. But there's a solution to their misguided thinking. If they're willing to change their mind and confess the opposite (that they *do* have sins), then there's hope.

Did you notice that this verse declares they'd be purified from *all* unrighteousness? The phrase *all unrighteousness* is reminiscent of forgiveness passages elsewhere in the epistles. Here, John isn't asking for a one-by-one tallying of our sins in order for Christians to stay forgiven and cleansed. That would be ludicrous, given the impossibility for any human to truly comply!

> You've already committed thousands of sins that you've forgotten about.

Think about it. You've already committed thousands of sins that you've forgotten about. You can't possibly remember them in order to confess them and become forgiven for them. That's why Christians have to be purified from *all* unrighteousness — once and for all!

This contextualized interpretation of verse 9 may be new to those of us who have viewed the passage as a prescription for Christians who just committed an individual sin. First John 1:9 has been a "bar of soap" routine to stay cleansed and in fellowship with God.

What a tragedy! In adopting this view, we fail to acknowledge that only blood (not words) brings forgiveness. We miss the fact that Jesus' once-for-all blood sacrifice brought lifelong cleansing. So we dialogue with God *to feel* forgiven and cleansed. This feeling serves as our confirmation that God just forgave us. But some aren't able to conjure up this feeling. And as a result they end up doubting their forgiveness!

CONFESSION CLARIFIED

Let's clarify an important point. The meaning of *confess* is "to say the same as" or "to agree." Believers should agree with God on all counts—not just about sins but about everything. Although we don't confess our sins *in order to receive* new portions of forgiveness and cleansing, we should still agree with God concerning the folly of sin. We're his children, and it is only his ways that fulfill. We're designed from the ground up to agree with him, depend on him, and live from him.

But it's equally important to recognize that we don't impel God or put him into motion through our confession. He's not waiting to dole out forgiveness or cleansing. We don't need to keep "short accounts" with God, since he has destroyed the record book!

God has taken away our sins. He remembers them no more. As believers, our forgiveness and cleansing aren't dependent on our memory, our confession, or our asking. Our forgiveness and cleansing are solely because of the finished work of Jesus Christ.

THE "OTHER" CONFESSION

What about James 5:16? James talks about confessing our sins to each other and praying for each other. But he's saying we should listen to each other's struggles, offer counsel where appropriate, and pray for each other. The context of James's exhortation to confess our sins to each other *has nothing to do with God's forgiving or cleansing us.*

Confession to trusted friends and to God is healthy. It's normal and natural to talk about your struggles with people who care about you. The indispensable truth to grasp, however, is that confession does *not* initiate cleansing in your life. We've already been cleansed "once for all" through the onetime blood sacrifice that needs no repeating.

Let's be honest about our struggles, but let's also be clear about what the cross accomplished. The Catholic goes to a priest, and the Protestant thinks he does better by appealing directly to God. But any system that doesn't factor in once-for-all forgiveness is intrinsically flawed.

God doesn't want us to think that human priests apportion forgiveness to us. Nor does he want us to envision his doling out forgiveness from heaven on a "first come, first serve" basis! Instead, he wants us to ascribe real meaning to Jesus' declaration, "It is finished."

> Any system that doesn't factor in once-for-all forgiveness is intrinsically flawed.

Only then will we turn from sins for the right reason. Our motivation shouldn't be to obtain forgiveness in return. We're already forgiven and cleansed children of the living God. Our motivation should be the fulfillment that comes from truly being ourselves.

23

THE REALITY IS THAT CHRISTIANS ARE TOTALLY FORGIVEN PEOPLE, whether we fully understand it or not. Realizing it simply allows us to cease our restless activity of trying to "get right" with God. Realizing it frees us to enjoy life free from guilt, as God intends —something that those under the Old could *never* do: "The worshipers would have been cleansed once for all, and would no longer have felt guilty for their sins" (Hebrews 10:2).

Within the last century, the term *fellowship* has evolved into a construct that Christians use to talk about feelings of closeness to God at a given time. It's a framework for relating to God that, unfortunately, we tend to develop from our interpersonal relationships. If we've sinned against a friend, family member, or coworker, we feel that our relationship with them is strained or broken until we apologize, are forgiven, and then restored to previous communication.

In the Scriptures, fellowship with God is *not* described in this way. Instead, a person is either in fellowship with God and therefore saved, or out of fellowship and therefore lost. In the ten instances of the word *fellowship* in the epistles, not once is there a moving "in and out of fellowship" with God based on recent performance.

Of course, we still mature spiritually. And when we sin,

consequences hit us. We can't escape the laws of the land. We also can't escape the reactions of others. If we sin against someone, we may experience difficult circumstances and our own disappointment with our choice. But we shouldn't mistake these earthly consequences for moving out of fellowship with God.

Our fellowship is stable and certain. God's face is always toward us. When we sin, he's there every step of the way to help us learn from our mistake. How arrogant it is to assume that we could escape sin alone, while out of fellowship, in order to get back in!

If we buy the lie that God sits in a swivel chair, ready to rotate his face away from us when we sin, then we proclaim a God of conditional love and conditional fellowship. But this is to ignore the work of Jesus, who on the cross cried out, "My God, my God, why have you forsaken me?" (Matthew 27:46). Jesus was out of fellowship with his Father so we would never be.

> Jesus was out of fellowship with his Father so we would never be.

However, sorrow over a wrongdoing is normal and expected in the Christian life. In fact, I'd be concerned about any person who was *not* sorry for their sins! There's a godly sorrow or regret over sins that leads a person to desire change (2 Corinthians 7:10). This regret occurs because believers are designed for good works, not sins. When we sin, we're not living out our destiny. When we sin, we won't be content with our choice.

We're meant for something greater.

We're meant to display the life of Jesus Christ.

Nothing less.

THE LORD'S PRAYER

Let's talk about the Lord's Prayer, in which Jesus taught his disciples to say, "Forgive us our sins" (Luke 11:4). This is a request—an asking for forgiveness. It is not a claiming of what one already has. So how does the Lord's Prayer fit in with once-for-all forgiveness?

We can't disregard the words of Jesus! But how do we *understand* his words, given that neither Paul nor Peter nor John—nor any other apostle—advocates asking for forgiveness as a daily routine for believers? The answer lies in examining the context of this prayer, its content, and its intended audience.

Jesus warns his followers to avoid meaningless repetition of lengthy prayers. He says babblers are not heard because of their many words (Matthew 6:7). So the disciples naturally want a model for "good" prayer. What we see today in many churches is the repetition of the same prayer Jesus offered the disciples. Yet do we even realize what we're praying?

Most Christians know that the Lord's Prayer contains an appeal for forgiveness. But Jesus tells his audience to ask God to forgive them *only to the same degree* that they've forgiven others.

> Jesus tells his audience to ask God to forgive them *only to the same degree* that they've forgiven others.

The prayer isn't merely, "Forgive us our debts." It's more specific than that. Jesus prays "Forgive us our debts, *as we also have forgiven our debtors*" (Matthew 6:12, italics added). This prayer might be paraphrased like this: "God, take a survey of my life and my track record as a forgiver. Then give me the same type and amount of forgiveness I've given to others."

What was the reaction of those who heard Jesus praying in this way? Did it excite them? Did it free them from guilt? Probably not. Jesus was deliberately showing his Jewish listeners the futility of seeking total forgiveness under the Old. If a person operates under a conditional religious system, they can only *receive what they earn* or give to others.

As with other harsh teachings of Jesus, some have tried to explain away the stringency of the Lord's Prayer. Some suggest that we Christians *are* forgiving people and therefore we *tend* to forgive others just like God does. So some claim there's no conflict between this prayer and passages in the epistles. But Jesus makes his intended meaning clear as he concludes the prayer, "For if you forgive others when they sin against you, your heavenly Father will also forgive you. *But if you do not forgive others their sins, your Father will not forgive your sins*" (Matthew 6:14–15, italics added).

Jesus is certainly not saying, "Since you are such a forgiving person ..." On the contrary, he's setting up a black-and-white condition for his listeners to be forgiven. They'll be forgiven if they forgive others. They won't be forgiven if they don't forgive others. In fact, they'll be forgiven *to the same degree* to which they forgive others.

Now compare these words with Paul's statement in Colossians 3:13. The apostle writes, "Forgive as the Lord *forgave* you" (italics added). The Lord's Prayer and Paul's exhortation are incompatible. Jesus is calling us to forgive *so that* we can be forgiven, while Paul calls us to forgive *because* we've already been forgiven.

According to Jesus' teaching, everything rests on our shoulders. We must forgive so that God will forgive us. According to Paul, God has already taken the initiative. We've already been forgiven, and we're called to pass it on.

So how can Jesus' teachings and Paul's teachings be in opposition to each other? Weren't they *both* teaching under the same New Covenant?

An Old Prayer

As we've already discussed, blood initiates a covenant. When Jesus taught Jews how to pray, his blood had not been shed yet. Therefore, the New had not begun. The Lord's Prayer is an Old

Covenant prayer taught to Jews before once-for-all forgiveness was accomplished.

But why would Jesus prescribe a formula for earning forgiveness through forgiving others? Perhaps for the same reason he told the rich man to sell all his possessions (Mark 10:21). Maybe for the same reason he told his Jewish hearers to gouge out their eyes and cut off their hands in their fight against sin (Matthew 5:29–30). Possibly for the same reason he implored Jews to be perfect just as their heavenly Father is perfect (Matthew 5:48).

> The Lord's Prayer is an Old Covenant prayer taught to Jews before once-for-all forgiveness was accomplished.

He said these things to bring despair, not hope.

What reaction would you have if you heard this teaching and sincerely wanted to follow it? Like the rich man, all who were honest about their chances at achieving *that* level of righteousness, dedication, and forgiveness went away disheartened. The rich man who earnestly sought truth confronted a painful reality. And the result was despondency.

Jesus spoke truth to every audience he encountered. Not all of Jesus' statements were intended to show the hopelessness of the Old. Jesus also prophesied about the beauty of the New: the kingdom of God, the role of the Holy Spirit, and his return, to name a few. But this prayer was meant to prepare those under the Old for the New. He illuminated the futility of their efforts to get right with God. The best method to redeem those who think they're on a good road is to bury them with standards that are just too great.

When people realize that the system they are under demands more than they can give, they're ready for something New.

24

GRADUATE SCHOOLS FEATURE FACULTY MEMBERS OF ALL KINDS. I'LL never forget my first semester when I met two gifted professors who each treated students very differently. One professor was stern and strict. As he walked the halls, the passers-by would tighten up. He was intimidating in his tone and condescending in his speech. The other professor treated his students as colleagues. He was friendly, full of energy, and encouraging toward those around him. He looked for opportunities to help his students succeed. Rather than pointing out their failures, he had a future-oriented focus: What would his students need to succeed? Would they be ready for placement in top-notch research institutions? He was interested in training them for what was ahead.

Both professors were well respected in their field. But they went about their daily interactions with students in starkly different ways. As students got to know both professors, you can imagine what happened. They were drawn to one and repelled by the other. I still remember the day we were required to select academic advisers to mentor us. Numerous students flocked to the kind professor. Very few, if any, wanted advising from the condescending professor.

The Holy Spirit is our mentor. But what type of mentor is he? What is his approach and how does he interact with us?

CONVICTION OR COUNSEL?

The book of Hebrews tells us that God (the Father) doesn't remember our sins anymore (Hebrews 8:12). Then the author reiterates the same point, declaring that *the Holy Spirit* doesn't remember our sins either (Hebrews 10:17). Why mention this point twice?

Sometimes we separate God's act of love on the cross from the Holy Spirit's perspective on sins. This subtly implies that God and the Holy Spirit are not on the same page. It's amazing that we can imagine ourselves to be at peace with God the Father, but then we think that the Holy Spirit is making us feel guilty and distant as punishment for our sins. Many Christians call this feeling the *conviction* of the Holy Spirit.

> We think that the Holy Spirit is making us feel guilty and distant as punishment for our sins.

How can we use the term *conviction* for Christians? In one breath, we admit that God has forgotten our sins. We say he doesn't take them into account. We may even agree with the writer of Hebrews that the Holy Spirit himself has forgotten our sins. But in the next breath, we announce firmly that the Holy Spirit *convicts* us of our sins.

To unravel this apparent contradiction, let's look at the meaning of the term *convict*.

Convict means "to find guilty." Within a judicial system, conviction is followed by sentencing and then punishment. Inside the word *conviction* is the term we usually reserve for a person who is incarcerated —a *convict*. So should the verb *convict* be used to describe interaction between the Holy Spirit and children of God? Probably not.

The root *convict-* only appears eight times in the Bible. And not one of those appearances has anything to do with the daily life of the believer! The gospel of John contains the only passage that joins *Holy Spirit* and *convict*:

> I [Jesus] tell you the truth, it is to your advantage that I
> go away; for if I do not go away, the Helper [Holy Spirit]
> will not come to you; but if I go, I will send Him to you.
> And He, when He comes, will *convict the world* concern-
> ing sin and righteousness and judgment; concerning sin,
> *because they do not believe in Me.*
>
> JOHN 16:7–9 NASB, italics added

So who's being convicted here? It's the world, characterized as *people who do not believe* in Jesus. Jesus is not talking about Christians who already believe in him! In this and all other relevant passages, context makes it clear that the term *convict* is exclusively reserved for unbelievers.

NEW EXPECTATIONS

If it's inaccurate to speak of the Holy Spirit as convicting believers, then what can we expect from him regarding our behavior? The epistles clearly describe how the Holy Spirit operates in the lives of believers. He's our Counselor, our Helper, our Comforter, our Advocate—and the one who guides us into all the truth (John 16:13). He prays on our behalf (Romans 8:26). And he testifies to us concerning our identity as children of God (Romans 8:16).

But how does our behavior improve? By these very means! How can we not believe that the counsel of the Holy Spirit is sufficient to bring about genuine change in our lives? Rather than dredging up the past, the Holy Spirit trains us for the future. Rather than treating us as convicts, he recognizes us as holy saints. When sinful behaviors occur in our lives, he reminds us of Jesus' work on the cross. We need to know that we're pure and made for good

It's inaccurate to speak of the Holy Spirit as convicting believers.

deeds, not sins. The world is certainly *not* going to teach us that!

The work of the Holy Spirit doesn't find a parallel in this world. We can't look to any other relationship as an example of his counsel and guidance. Why not? Because no human mentor can maintain a mind-set of total forgiveness, esteem us as perfect people, and simultaneously coach us regarding attitudes and actions.

Is this just splitting hairs? Not at all. Too many Christians succumb to the Accuser while wrongly attributing these attacks to the *conviction* of the Holy Spirit. There's no better tactic for Satan than to first tempt us and then flood us with guilt by masquerading as the Holy Spirit. Sometimes we even entertain guilt just for having the thought pass through our minds!

God has forgotten our sins. Shouldn't we? When our view of God is off-kilter or our understanding of Christ's work is incomplete, it's natural that our sense of what the Holy Spirit is doing will likewise be askew.

We've got a clean slate. The Holy Spirit is in our corner. He'll *never* leave us. And he is an effective coach.

God has forgotten our sins. Shouldn't we?

25

SO THERE YOU ARE, AND ALL OF YOUR FRIENDS ARE WATCHING as every mean, petty, and selfish act you've ever done is projected on the big heavenly movie screen. As soon as the movie is over, you're really gonna get it. But maybe the most embarrassing part is how long the film seems to be lasting! "Could we maybe pause for an intermission or something?" you ask. But no one laughs, because many are just too horrified. And others are too busy worrying that the next feature might be their own blockbuster film.

The concept of final judgment seems to contradict total forgiveness, and the idea of all our sins being projected on a movie screen for review by Almighty God fills us with insecurity. So how can we reconcile the scriptural certainty of a "great white throne" judgment (Revelation 20:11) with our once-for-all forgiveness?*

THE GREAT WHITE TRUTH

The events surrounding the great white throne are recounted in Revelation 20 and 21. Revelation 20:11–15 informs us that God calls "the dead" to his throne for judgment—those who are pulled up from the sea, death, and Hades. They are judged

---

*See Sidelight 10 on pp. 235–36.

according to their deeds and then hurled into the lake of fire. There's one criterion that dooms them: their names aren't written in the book of life.

Chapter 21 then addresses the church. Here God calls believers his "bride" and says there'll be no sorrow for us in heaven. So we see a clear distinction made between the dead pulled up from hell in chapter 20 and Christ's precious bride in chapter 21. The bottom line is that Christians won't be put on trial and judged, since we believe in the Lord Jesus Christ and our names are written in the book of life.

Christians won't be put on trial and judged.

One eye-opening statement concerning our perfect standing before the Judge is made by Jesus himself: *"He who believes in [Jesus] is not judged;* he who does not believe has been judged already, because he has not believed in the name of the only begotten Son of God"* (John 3:18 NASB, italics added).

Despite the clarity of God's Word, I've heard some use the final judgment to instill what they term "godly fear" in believers. I've even heard some say that they determine the quality of a sermon by how guilty they feel afterward! Taken out of context, the great white throne judgment can seriously damage our sense of assurance.

CONVEYOR BELT

Picture an assembly line at the Ford Motor Company. It's your first real job, and you and a coworker are busily assembling fuel injectors intended for the Ford Mustang. The first week on the job, the conveyor belt seemed to move so quickly, but now you're getting used to it. Now that weeks and months have passed, building fuel injectors feels like second nature.

Of course, you've made your share of mistakes, and farther down the assembly line the product of your errors have been discarded, melted down, and recast for future use. But as time passes, you learn to make fewer and fewer errors, and the process begins to feel somewhat natural. In fact, you sometimes find yourself assembling dozens of injectors without even realizing the time is passing!

Understandably, Ford is interested in quality work. So an inspector comes by to assess your team's work and carefully take note of the waste product as well as the number of fully functioning injectors you've assembled. Sure, some of your coworkers get a bit nervous when the inspector is around, but you've got an ace in the hole. You live with the inspector! He's still "Dad" to you. And he has always sought to teach you the tricks of the trade, ever since you were little and would tag along with "Daddy" at work.

Observe that you and your coworkers aren't on the conveyor belt. Neither your dad nor Ford Motor Company has any interest in judging you as a person! Only the *product* of your work — whether of high quality or not — is on the belt. Similarly, Jesus informs us that those who believe in him are *not* judged. But our works are tested, assessed, or appraised as they proceed down the conveyor belt toward God's collection of his Son's accomplishments. Paul speaks of our works being tested to see if they'll endure:

> The Father wants to showcase all that his Son has accomplished.

> No one can lay any *foundation* other than the one already laid, which is *Jesus Christ.* If anyone builds on this foundation using gold, silver, costly stones, wood, hay or straw, their work will be shown for what it is, because the Day will bring it to light. It will be revealed with fire, and the fire will *test the quality of each person's work.*
>
> 1 CORINTHIANS 3:11–13, italics added

The principle is simple: Anything built on Christ will stand the test of time; anything done in fleshly effort will not. But *you* are never on trial. *You* are not on the conveyor belt.

This is a crucial distinction to make, since many Christians aren't clear on it. God has divorced who we are from what we've done, so that our destiny and standing are *not* in question. At the same time, the Father wants to showcase all that his Son has accomplished. And there'll be a grand celebration at the end of time as we know it.

HEAVENLY MERCHANDISE

"OK, so maybe we ourselves are not going to be judged, but I still want to earn tons of rewards in heaven!" Quite often I'll hear a statement like this after teaching on our freedom from God's judgment.

As humans, we always seem to be looking for a punishment- or reward-based motivation to keep our behavior on track. While we're more apt to dismiss a blatant guilt motivation, the picture often painted is that God will be doling out mansions of various sizes and other merit-based awards when we hit heaven. Christians have commonly used the term *rewards* to refer to extra square footage or certificates redeemable for crowns and jewels in heaven's gift shop.

> The term *rewards* does not appear anywhere in the New Testament.

In reality, the term *rewards* does not appear anywhere in the New Testament. The apostle Paul speaks of a "reward" (singular, not plural) or a "prize" in the context of running a race and reaching the end. But Paul also notes that everything else is like garbage next to knowing Christ Jesus (Philippians 3:8). Given this truth, do we really believe that God will be awarding larger homes and nicer jewelry to those who depended on Jesus more?

God doesn't want us to think and act in certain ways because we're seeking to accumulate heavenly merchandise. Just as Paul was willing to lose all things for the sake of knowing Christ, we too should make it our agenda to know him. For more wealth in heaven? No, we want to know him simply because it's the greatest thing going on planet Earth.

TREASURE HUNT

But doesn't Jesus himself tell us to store up treasures in heaven (Matthew 6:20)? Yes, but treasures aren't rewards. People *discover* treasures. They don't earn them. Once a treasure is discovered, it can be abandoned or it can be stored somewhere.

When God tells us we can store up treasures in heaven, he's asking us to consider our daily choices and their outcomes. Some choices end in a worthless product that is later burned up like wood, hay, or straw. Other choices endure for eternity since they are expressions of Jesus Christ.

Essentially, God is posing the following questions: Given who you are and what you know, what will you invest in? Will you store up attitudes and actions that endure forever, or will you pursue dead works that end up being burned?

The choice is ours.

PART 6

we don't marry dead people

If you will but trust Christ, not only for the death he died in order to redeem you, but also for the life that he lives and waits to live through you, the very next step you take will be a step taken in the very energy and power of God himself.

Major W. Ian Thomas (1914–2007)

26

I'm a careful shopper. One of the things I hate the most is buying a "lemon." I'll often spend dozens of hours researching brands and models before I make a purchase. Whether it's audio-visual equipment, golf clubs, or automobiles, I usually examine a detailed set of specifications, product tests, and consumer ratings to determine performance and reliability. It's gotten to the point that friends and family members will call me before they buy for themselves. My wife jokes that I should open a consulting business for everyday shoppers, but *Consumer Reports* has already beaten me to the punch.

WHAT *BRAND* OF LIFE?

The Scriptures work hard at communicating that the life offered to us is both reliable and guaranteed. In short, it's no lemon. It's top-rated, with the best warranty in the business.

The word *eternal* is often used to express the endurance of the life we have in Jesus. Many equate eternal life with everlasting life, but these two phrases don't carry the same meaning. The term *eternal life* is curious, because it means life with no end *and no beginning*. Keep this in mind as you read these thoughts on eternal life:

> And this is the testimony: God has given us eternal life, and *this life is in his Son*. Whoever *has the Son has life*; whoever does not have the Son of God does not have life.
>
> I write these things to you who believe in the name of the Son of God so that you may know that you have eternal life.
>
> 1 John 5:11–13, italics added

Who is the only person whose life had *no beginning*? Then if you have eternal life, *whose* life do you possess? Eternal life doesn't primarily involve heaven, church services, or even the Bible. Eternal life is not merely a better life or a better purpose for life. It's an altogether different life. It's *God's life*. Here we don't reference religious notions. Instead, we're discussing Eden matters.

> Eternal life doesn't primarily involve heaven, church services, or even the Bible.

If there were no church buildings, no Bible studies, and no other saints on the planet, you'd still need eternal life. If you were stranded on a deserted island, you'd still need eternal life. The essence of the gospel meets that basic need. The fundamental promise within the New is divine life restored within humanity.

BOOK KNOWLEDGE?

In order to grasp what it means to possess life, it's helpful to divorce it from what we typically term *church*. For example, one hindrance to understanding the real gospel as life restoration is an obsession with "book knowledge."

Don't get me wrong—I love the Word of God. And this book is centered on highlighting spiritual truths from the Bible. But we must be careful that we don't master the Book without getting to know the Author. What does it really matter if we're expert scholars in biblical studies and know nothing of displaying true life? Jesus warns us not to get puffed up with book knowledge about spiritual matters:

> *You study the Scriptures diligently* because you think that in them you possess eternal life. These are the very Scriptures that testify about me, *yet you refuse to come to me to have life.*
>
> JOHN 5:39–40, italics added

Jesus' statement allows us to see an important truth laid bare: the life of Jesus in us is what matters most. We shouldn't assume that someone who studies the Bible for a living is a new creation. In addition, we shouldn't equate "Bible smarts" with spiritual maturity. They're certainly *not* one and the same. In fact, far from it! As in Jesus' day, it's often those who are puffed up about their good handle on what the Scriptures *say* (not what they mean!) who resist the counsel of the Holy Spirit.

DAD'S "TESTIMONY"

"I don't know what I'm going to say!" my father whispered as he stood up to address the church crowd. "You'll think of something," my mother answered. My mother had only been a Christian a short time, but my father was not yet in Christ. Nevertheless, the pastor of the church they attended had invited my father to present his testimony on a Sunday morning.

My father was an attorney, businessman, and politician. He carried some weight in the northern Virginia area where my family lived. Perhaps for this reason, the pastor had selected him to address the crowd and give his testimony. Really, my dad had nothing to say. He wasn't in Christ and didn't even understand the path to salvation.

As my dad concluded his testimony, the audience clapped and cheered. After the service, many came forward to shake his hand and congratulate him on a fine testimony.

So what did my father say? In short, his testimony was about the importance of faith, church life, and raising children in a Christian environment. He told the people how important they were to him because of their love for and support of our family. This brought the applause and the compliments. There was no mention of the work of Jesus Christ. Nothing about accepting Jesus' life. Just rhetoric about the importance of church, faith, and Christian values. It wasn't until a year later that my father became a new creation in Christ.

I share this true story with you to illustrate how Christians are sometimes unable to discern the difference between spiritual truth and fine-sounding religious talk. I think this story also shows how some can fully believe, as my dad did, that they're in the church when they're not really *in* Christ.

Though some may be active in church activities, volunteering left and right, and even giving eloquent teachings on the importance of faith and Christian living, it doesn't mean a new birth has taken place. We shouldn't lose sight of the importance of heart surgery. Without God's internal surgery, any outward expression of churchiness is a waste of time and energy. After all, there are more interesting things to do with our time than to play church!

> We shouldn't lose sight of the importance of heart surgery.

It's sobering to realize that approximately 80 to 90 percent of the early church couldn't read or write. This means they didn't do personal Bible study or keep up with the most recent Christian literature. Despite their illiteracy, these believers were used to spread the gospel rapidly throughout the world. They were tortured, stoned, and killed for their faith, and they willingly submitted their testimonies to those who sought to crush them.

How did they manage to become such strong Christians without a daily "quiet time" in the Word? Sure, we're fortunate to have God's Word at our fingertips today. But studying the Bible alone is no substitute for possessing and displaying life — the same life that members of the early church possessed.

More Than the Cross

Eternal life is Jesus' life. Jesus declared himself to be "the resurrection and the life" and "the way and the truth and the life" (John 11:25; 14:6). He also stated, "Because I live, you also will live" (John 14:19). Clearly, our eternal life is tied up in him. Our new spiritual life is actually his life.

So we don't have a spiritual gift package awaiting us in heaven. We have Jesus Christ in us right now. In fact, it's his life that *saves* us. We recognize the importance of Jesus' blood for our forgiveness. But Jesus' death *alone* isn't sufficient to save us! His death on the cross doesn't provide the life we need. It is actually Jesus' resurrection that saves us:

> If, while we were God's enemies, we were *reconciled to him through the death* of his Son, how much more, having been reconciled, shall we be *saved through his life*!
>
> ROMANS 5:10, italics added

I don't believe we should separate the work of Jesus into individual events and treat them as though they occurred independently of one other. After all, there would be no resurrection without his death. But there's an important point here: Jesus' blood doesn't bring us new life. Blood brings forgiveness of sins, nothing more. Therefore, we shouldn't be satisfied with understanding the meaning of the cross alone. We should insist that there's more than

> We should insist that there's more than forgiveness alone.

forgiveness alone. And we find what we seek through an understanding of the *resurrection* and what it means for us personally.

PAINTER OF LIFE

Many Christians struggle to articulate what the resurrection means to them personally. I've asked groups of Christians what the resurrection means to them and usually don't get a response beyond the statement that it demonstrated God's power over death. Is this all there is? Paul stated that if there is no resurrection, then his whole message is meaningless and we're to be pitied for our beliefs (1 Corinthians 15:12–19)! There has to be more to the resurrection than God's showing off his power. God has already shown off through creation, the flood, fulfilled prophecies, miracles, and even the resurrection of Lazarus from the dead.

Fortunately, there *is* more to the resurrection. The life we possess within us is not Jesus the Man who lived, taught, and died after thirty-three years on earth. Sure, that's part of his track record. But the life housed within us is the risen Christ, who now sits right beside God. Hence, we're not being asked to imitate the recorded actions of Jesus of Nazareth. Instead, we're invited to allow Jesus to do what he has always done—be himself. The risen Christ wants to do this through our unique personalities in every moment of every day.

Imagine billions of unique canvases throughout history—different sizes, shapes, and textures. The Master Painter wants to paint expressions of himself on your life. You might say, "Who am I to display God's life?" But God wants to make his mark on your life with beautiful brushstrokes that only he can fashion together to create a masterpiece. Although God has painted his heart out countless times throughout history, he jealously desires to do it all over again on *your* canvas and my canvas.

Somehow it is quality art in a different style every time.

27

Let me tell you a story. Consider Steve and Andrea, who dated throughout college and had recently become engaged. When they invited their pastor to conduct their marriage ceremony, he was honored to be a part of their special day. They were so perfect for each other, and everyone knew it.

But then, just one day before the wedding, Steve fell to the ground and died instantly of a heart attack. He had no history of heart trouble and had showed no signs leading up to his shocking death. The most difficult aspect of the whole event was not his passing but how Andrea sought to cope with it.

Although Steve already seemed to be dead, the medical team rushed him to the hospital. Andrea rode along in the ambulance, but by the time they reached the hospital, it was obvious there was no hope. Their pastor met up with Andrea in the emergency room, and the first words that left her mouth were, "I still want to marry him! I don't care if he's gone. I still love him. And we're going to go through with this." At that point, their pastor didn't know what to say.

Twenty-four hours later, the time for the wedding had arrived, and Andrea still hadn't changed her mind. She insisted that everything should continue as scheduled. What was to be a wedding would now become a combination funeral-wedding. For the first time ever, the pastor was conducting two ceremonies simultaneously. His instructions were to officially commit Steve's body to burial and then to announce Steve and Andrea as husband and wife. Out of concern for Andrea, he agreed to do both.

As the ceremony began, half of the audience was saddened by Steve's passing. At the same time, Andrea's side of the church shed tears of joy over her union with Steve. And the pastor was caught in the middle, not knowing how to feel. And the most awkward moment of all was when Andrea leaned into the coffin to kiss her groom and then fell inside!

Every bit of this story is pure fiction. But by telling it, I want to illustrate an important point: we don't marry dead people. To do so would be quite strange. But aren't we the bride of Jesus Christ? And he lived two thousand years ago. Are we *spiritually* married to a dead person? Obviously, the answer is no. It's important to understand that we're joined to the risen Christ, not to a dead religious teacher.

Some Christians mistakenly obsess over everything that the historical Jesus did in the four gospels. We memorize his words and actions and try to imitate them the best we can. When we think of being the bride of Christ, we may imagine ourselves to only be married to Jesus of Nazareth—the God-man who lived a "good" life for thirty-three years. But the Scriptures indicate that we're married to an eternal, risen Christ.

Although we were once married to the law, we obtained a "divorce" through our death. Now we're reborn and remarried to a heavenly husband. And our union with him will last forever:

> So, my brothers and sisters, you also died to the law through the body of Christ, that you might *belong to another, to him who was raised from the dead*, in order that we might bear fruit for God.
>
> ROMANS 7:4, italics added

Everything we need is found in our spiritual husband, Jesus Christ. Once we are married to him, we no longer have to wait or hope or even ask for spiritual resources. We already have everything we need for planet Earth right here and now.

So we're not merely married to a part of Christ or to his teachings. We're spiritually united with *all* of him. He doesn't swoop down out of heaven at special times to give us counsel. Instead, the entirety of Christ himself is joined to us twenty-four hours a day, seven days a week, without interruption.

FULLNESS

In Colossians, Paul reveals the amazing truth that we possess *all* of Christ within us: "In Christ all the fullness of the Deity lives in bodily form, and in Christ *you have been brought to fullness*. He is the head over every power and authority" (Colossians 2:9–10, italics added).

Fullness means that we're not missing any part of the person of Christ. In Christ we have what we need for *life* and godliness (2 Peter 1:3). This doesn't mean we merely have what we need to understand the Bible or what's required to conduct a church service. God has given us much more. In Christ we find everything we need for normal, everyday life. God knows the resources needed for life here on earth, and it's all included in the life we possess through Christ:

> His divine power has given us everything we need for a
> godly life through our knowledge of him who called us
> by his own glory and goodness.
>
> 2 PETER 1:3

The realization that we already have *everything* in Christ Jesus impacts our approach to daily living. If we merely had a ticket to heaven, there'd be no power to live in the present.

FULFILLMENT

Sometimes we attempt to live a godly life in the hope of earning rewards in heaven. But it's very difficult, if not totally unrealistic, to live for something far off in the future. Although the idea of living to earn future rewards might sound practical from a natural perspective, it's simply not rooted in God's Word. The motivation for daily living within the New Testament centers around acting like the person you truly are and benefiting from Christ's life in the here and now.

Paul urges believers to walk in a manner worthy of their calling (Ephesians 4:1). In Romans, he highlights the teaching that there's no benefit to sin and that the outcome of those things is death (Romans 6:21–23). At no time are we told to live an upright life in order to garner a more righteous standing or to collect prizes in heaven. Quite the opposite! We're urged to grasp an important spiritual truth: when we come to Jesus Christ, we receive his life. Through our expression of him, we find fulfillment.

> When we come to Jesus Christ, we receive his life.

AN ANCIENT CONVERSATION

It's possible to hear something so often that you grow numb to the words and the significance behind them. The term *born again* has been used and at times abused to the point that many have become callous to its real meaning. Yet there's a valuable truth to be discovered in it. After all, these are Jesus' own words!

Here's an ancient conversation between Jesus and a local expert in the law:

Jesus replied, "Very truly I tell you, no one can see the kingdom of God without being born again."

"How can anyone be born when they are old?" Nicodemus asked. "Surely they cannot enter a second time into their mother's womb to be born!"

Jesus answered, "Very truly I tell you, no one can enter the kingdom of God without being born of water and the Spirit. Flesh gives birth to flesh, but the Spirit gives birth to spirit."

JOHN 3:3–6

First, let's do away with a commonly held notion about this passage. This conversation has nothing to do with baptism in H_2O. Here Jesus is talking about two births that are necessary in order to enter the kingdom. The first is a natural birth, meaning a person is born as an infant from a human mother. The second is a spiritual birth. The natural birth is described in two ways: "born of water" and "flesh gives birth to flesh." The spiritual birth is also described in two ways: "born of . . . the Spirit" and "the Spirit gives birth to spirit."

Some have used this passage to support the idea of "no salvation without water baptism," but nothing could be further from the truth. Jesus is saying that an infant is naturally housed in water within the womb of his mother. On his 0th birthday, he's born of water. After placing his faith in Jesus Christ, he's literally born a second time spiritually. God issues to him a new human spirit, and God's own Spirit comes to reside in him. The claim that one must be dunked in the local swimming hole in order to obtain spiritual rebirth is not supported by the context of the passage.

Childbirth is an amazing event. I'll never forget the day I witnessed the birth of our son, Gavin. What was so amazing was that something appeared to come from nothing. A human being with all of his complexity was formed from a sperm and an egg inside a sphere of water over a period of nine months.

I remember all that my wife went through — the morning sickness, the labor pains, and the joy that broke forth at the birth. Experiencing this firsthand gave me new insight into the Holy Spirit's "giving birth" to us spiritually. There's something remarkable to be learned from Jesus' description of salvation as being born of the Spirit. If God literally birthed us through his Spirit, what does that say about our spiritual "genetics"?

> God literally birthed us through his Spirit.

THE PARADOX OF LIGHT

At the turn of the century, physicists were researching light to determine its nature. Some published evidence that light was a *particle*, while others experimented with light and determined it was a *wave*. When light is shone through narrow slits, for example, it produces wavelike patterns similar to what we see in ocean water. But when light is shone at protons or electrons, it collides with these particles and bounces off like a billiard ball. Thus, it behaves like a particle.

Despite these conflicting findings, I'm happy to enlighten you about the nature of light. Is light a particle or a wave? The answer, quite definitively, is *yes*. Yes, light is a particle *and* a wave. Somehow it's both at the same time. From one perspective, it appears to be a particle. At the same time, further examination reveals that it's a wave.

Like the mystery of light, the outworking of our spiritual life can be equally perplexing. Is it supposed to be *Christ* in me working through me? Or is it *me* — who I am in Christ — working out my daily life? The answer, again, is *yes*.

Just as light is both a particle and a wave, it's both Christ in us *and* our own selves who live the Christian life. It's inaccurate to say that it's all Christ and that we act as hollow tubes. It's also inaccurate to envision the Christian life as a focus on identity alone —that we work things out on our own. Instead, it's a spiritual union—a mystery that was hidden and has now been

> It's a spiritual union — a mystery that was hidden and has now been revealed.

revealed. We're united together with Christ. He's our source of strength, and we're new, righteous, and compatible with him as our resource.

Is it him, or is it us? *Yes*, it's both.

28

NATURE AND NURTURE ARE TWO VERY DIFFERENT CONCEPTS. Scientists work to discover whether certain characteristics and behaviors within species are due to nature or nurture. Within many churches today, it appears we are emphasizing *nurture* as the means to spiritual growth. We're told we should focus on nurture through small groups, personal Bible study, accountability groups, and special events that spur us on to new commitments.

Of course, some of these things can be helpful. But do you see what I see? The Bible talks about considering ourselves dead to sin and realizing that God has raised us up and seated us with him (Romans 6:11; Ephesians 2:6). In light of these truths about our nature, we're told to not let sin reign and to set our minds on things above (Romans 6:12; Colossians 3:2). This is *not* nurture talk; this is nature talk!

> The church today often functions like any other morality-focused social group.

Too often, I see the church today functioning like any other morality-focused social group. It's time for us to wake up and realize that being born of the Spirit means we possess an amazing life within us. Because we're *already* different on the inside, we can live differently on the outside.

FROM START TO FINISH

We humans are quick to change strategies. If an approach doesn't satisfy quickly, we opt for another way. After the salvation experience, some of us grow impatient with God's natural plan for growth and fall prey to alternate means of "maturing." But the genuine path to growth is quite clear: *"Just as you received* Christ Jesus as Lord, *continue to live your lives* in him" (Colossians 2:6, italics added).

So how did we receive Christ Jesus? By hearing truth and believing it. Then how do we grow in him? Again, through *exposure* to truth and continually *setting our minds* on truth.

Simple, isn't it? If so, then why are these things so often neglected as the path to growth? Perhaps because they're *too* simple. Nearly two thousand years ago, the apostle Paul was worried that believers would stray from the simplicity of the message and turn toward another gospel — one that was really no gospel at all. He'd have that same concern for the church today.

The message of "Jesus plus nothing" from start to finish is often too humbling for us to swallow. Instead, we opt for performance hoops to jump through in order to impress God. Sure, we trust him alone for salvation and a place in heaven. But when it comes to daily living, it's difficult to fathom that he wants to be our resource and carry the load.

> The message of "Jesus plus nothing" is too humbling for many to swallow.

IN REMEMBRANCE

Growth doesn't happen by trying harder. It doesn't occur by a "two steps forward and one step back" approach. Genuine growth occurs as we absorb truth about who we *already* are and what we *already* possess in Christ.

Believers shouldn't passively sit around waiting to receive something new—more cleansing, more of the Holy Spirit, or more of whatever popular teaching says is lacking in us. We have everything we need for a godly life. We have an unshakable kingdom, an eternal covenant, and every spiritual blessing. We are complete and lack nothing. The only logical response is to spend our lives reminding each other of these extraordinary truths and giving thanks to our God.

Requesting and possessing are polar opposites. Once a person is in Christ, they are a possessor, not a requester. We see this point illustrated in the Lord's Supper. We shouldn't participate in this celebration in order to obtain something. Instead, we are to celebrate the Lord's Supper *in remembrance* of Jesus Christ. Just as this celebration is based solely on the work of Christ, we should conduct all of our business in the light of what he has already done.

To thank God for every spiritual blessing and then to ask him for more patience, for example, is to ignore Christ within us. Isn't patience part of what we need for a godly life? Do we have all the patience we need already implanted within us or don't we? Through the Scriptures, God answers this question with a resounding yes. Because we possess Christ himself, and since Christ is not lacking in patience, we already have all we need.

PUT GOD FIRST?

I find it somewhat amusing when I hear the phrase *put God first*. What would take second place? God first, country second, and family third? Although other things may be important to us, Jesus doesn't belong on a list with other items. He holds a status all his own. Since he is "our life" (Colossians 3:4 NIV), he's with us, in us, joined to us, and present in all aspects of our lives. He's everything to us: "To me, to live is Christ and to die is gain" (Philippians 1:21).

Notice that the apostle doesn't say that Christ is important to him. He says that "to live is Christ." Paul is not trying to give Christ a proper place among other things. Instead, he is recognizing the fact that Christ *is* everything to him. We may nod our heads in agreement, saying, "Yes, Christ is everything to me." But do we grasp the truth that Christ resides just beneath our humanity? That he is actually fused to our own person? Here Paul captures our attention with some radical statements:

> I have been crucified with Christ and I no longer live, but Christ lives in me. The life I now live in the body, I live by faith in the Son of God, who loved me and gave himself for me.
>
> GALATIANS 2:20

Paul claims that he participated in a crucifixion of sorts, and as a result Christ now lives in him. Many people make this claim out to be either symbolic if true or insane and untrue. But to claim anything short of this is to adopt a partial gospel. The very core of the New is that through Christ we receive what we lost through Adam, namely, the literal presence of the divine.

Christ resides just beneath our humanity.

This is *real* Christianity. A promise of heaven is not restoration of life. Studying a book written by God himself is still not restoration of life. Attending weekly gatherings in a building is not restoration of life. Even changing one's behavior in dramatic ways is not restoration of life. Of course, these things may *result* from restoration of life. But they're certainly not the means to life, nor are they a confirmation of the experience of life. Restoration of life occurs when God himself, through the person of Christ, resides within us.

Anything short of this is weak religiosity.

CLASSICAL GUITAR

When I registered for my last semester in college, I needed just a few more credits to graduate. In order to impress the girl I was dating, I decided to sign up for a classical guitar course. For sure, one thing I'm *not* is a musician.

"It can't be that hard," I thought to myself. Well, was I in for a surprise! My guitar instructor gave me one assignment for the semester—to play the introduction to "Dust in the Wind." This would be my final exam, so I practiced all semester. Day after day, I practiced the patterns, moving my fingers as quickly and accurately as I could.

After months of practice, the day arrived for my final exam. I walked in, guitar in hand, and sat down to play. About ten seconds into the song, I lost my place and had to start over. I began again at the beginning, since that was how I had memorized the finger movements. About ten seconds into the song, I was stumped once again. I simply couldn't remember which string to pluck next. During two more attempts, the same thing occurred. Finally I gave up. I thanked the professor for all her help during the semester and walked out.

As I made my way back to my car, tears of frustration streamed down my face. No matter how hard I tried, I was no guitarist. Music simply wasn't in me. I could make a faint attempt through mechanical movements, but playing the guitar just didn't come naturally.

I share my sad encounter with the classical guitar to illustrate a point: If we approach the Christian life in a mechanical way, trying to imitate the actions of Jesus in the gospels, we'll inevitably fail. The "What would Jesus do?" philosophy is not the same as the "Christ in you" approach. We're called to look within, to discover the life that is instinctive to us as new creations, and to live *from* that life. Imitating the *actions* of others, even the Jesus of the gospels, is nothing but a shallow, mechanical act that is not reliable under pressure. Just as all my pattern practice with the guitar ultimately failed me, merely going through the motions of imitating Christian activity pales in comparison to the experience of having Christ's life naturally flow from your personality.

> Imitating the *actions* of others, even the Jesus of the gospels, is nothing but a shallow, mechanical act.

Unlike my experience with the classical guitar, the good news for us is that we're "musical." We are partakers of the divine nature (2 Peter 1:4). And Christ's life through us is a natural fit.

THE MYSTERY

If you're spiritually joined to Christ, you've entered into a mystery. This mystery is the fullness of the gospel. Any message that fails to communicate this mystery falls short of the gospel. This mystery wasn't known for thousands of years under the Old, but it's been revealed in the New:

> I have become [the church's] servant by the commission God gave me to present to you the word of God in its fullness—*the mystery* that has been *kept hidden* for ages and generations, but is now disclosed to the Lord's people.
>
> COLOSSIANS 1:25–26, italics added

What could be more mysterious than participating in the divine nature? Through spiritual union with Christ, this mystery becomes a reality for us:

> To [the Lord's people] God has chosen to make known among the Gentiles the glorious riches of this mystery, which is *Christ in you*, the hope of glory.
>
> COLOSSIANS 1:27, italics added

It's frustrating to operate under a counterfeit belief system and not know why it fails you. I know, because I've been there. But the message of "Christ in you" is the real thing—the word of God in its *fullness*.

Today's alternative is a message that's an inaccurate part of the whole. All around us, we're inundated with a lackluster gospel that advocates partial forgiveness, a pressure-filled motivation for behavior change, and the promise of earned rewards in heaven or a cash return while on earth. This counterfeit is the reason that the church sometimes doesn't appear much different from the world. It's time for us to start over, if necessary, and seek the real thing.

Jesus Christ *in* us as our resource for everyday life is our only hope for any real change.

29

OF COURSE, SOMETIMES WE STILL TURN DEPENDENCY ON THE indwelling Christ into an opportunity to self-examine and introspect. And this isn't any better than any other religious move: "Am I abiding? What do I need to do to abide better?"

The term *abide*, I've noticed, is often used by those who seek something to do in order to maintain the reality of Christ living through them. The word *abide* simple means "to live," and Christ *already* lives in Christians! Some have made it out to be something beyond what Jesus intended it to be. Christ abiding in us is a truth, not a command for us to keep up our end of some bargain. Of course there are moment-by-moment choices to walk by faith, but the religion of "I must *get* Christ to abide in me" is a self-focus that is *not* the intention of the New. For this reason, I think it's valuable to address some issues related to the actual phenomenon of Christ living through us.

A KNOWING

If you've received Christ, then he lives in you, no matter what. Whether or not he lives through you in a given moment is simply a choice away. The Holy Spirit doesn't overpower you or circumvent your will. Instead, he wants you to respond to his counsel. As he counsels you and you respond to that counsel, Christ is living through you. It's simple, not complicated. In fact, the entire inner workings of your being are geared for this reality to occur. As you allow Christ to counsel you and express himself through your personality, you're fulfilling your destiny.

Christ living through you is not a feeling. It's not an emotional experience that you pursue. Having Christ live through you is really about knowing who you are and being yourself. Since Christ is your life, your source of true fulfillment, you'll only be content when you are expressing him. As you express him, you also express who God has made you to be.

God doesn't override us. However, God hasn't left us to our own devices to cope with life and be godly. Either of these extremes can harm our understanding of the gospel. God wants us to know that his Son works in us, through us, and alongside us since we're spiritually joined to him. Having Christ live through us begins with knowing that his life resides in us.

> Christ living through you is not a feeling.

In all of this, we're talking about a *knowing*, not a feeling.

JUST LIKE YOU

To everyone else, it'll just look like you. And it should look like you! Don't expect people to run up to you and ask a lot of questions because they notice how much you're like Jesus. When some people think of Jesus Christ, they hold a certain picture in their minds. It may have little or nothing to do with what the Holy Spirit is working in you.

Paul tells us that the treasure of Christ's life is in "jars of clay" so that we will be reminded that God is the source, not us

(2 Corinthians 4:7). Some may notice that we have an overall sense of peace or rest in our lives. They may also notice that we respond to some circumstances in an unusual manner. Or they may not notice anything at all. The popular teaching that everybody's watching and that we live in glass houses doesn't jibe with reality. The reality is that most people are busy thinking about themselves! However, you are well aware of the life that you carry within, and that is what is most important.

WITHIN OUR COMFORT ZONES

The idea that "Christ through me" could be frightening is rooted in a faulty sense of God's character. What's not to like about a God who is always for us and doesn't hold anything against us? If we're hesitant to relinquish our daily lives to God, it's because we don't yet trust his goodness.

Sure, we may know that God is good. But "God is always good *to me*" is an altogether different thought. Our fear of depending fully on Christ may also stem from not realizing that he thoroughly enjoys us. He has no desire to erase our uniqueness and turn us into clones. He considers our hobbies, interests, and senses of humor, and he wants to work through these in the expression of his life.

> "God is always good *to me*" is an altogether different thought.

I often hear it quite loudly proclaimed that we need God to take us out of our comfort zones. Certainly, the Christian life is no promise of smooth sailing and easy circumstances. But it's important to know that we've been rebuilt to display God. "Christ through us" lies *within* our comfort zones. We're made for expression of him, and anything else is unnatural and uncomfortable for us.

To *WILL* and Do

God won't make us do things we don't want to do. Instead, the Bible tells us that God works in us to will (want) and to act in order to fulfill his good purpose (Philippians 2:13). This means we'll genuinely want what God wants. If it's not placed on our hearts, it's not of him.

God works through our hearts and minds to cause us to walk in his ways. He's not asking us to live a life we don't want to live. On the contrary, he has placed Christ's desires within us, and we're only satisfied as we fulfill them. Whether we realize it or not, our greatest desire is to express Christ in every moment.

Sometimes when people hear the term *surrender*, they imagine their entire lives hanging in the balance as they decide whether or not to go on the mission field. This idea is misleading, since most believers need to settle in and know Christ in their current circumstances rather than trying to alter them. Although some may end up changing their vocation or the place they live, most of God's children are intended for a setting they already know.

Are you open to Christ living through your current, everyday life? Or must he change your circumstances for you to believe that he can live through you? We must grasp that Christ is compatible with our humanity, no matter where we live and no matter what our daily lives involve.

> Jesus demonstrated that humanity is capable of displaying the divine.

One reason that Jesus was born as a baby and lived for thirty-three years in genuine human flesh was to demonstrate that humanity is capable of displaying the divine.

LOOK FOR EVIDENCE?

Of course, the idea of Jesus living through your personality can lead to a measuring of sorts. Sometimes people become introspective about the whole thing: "Am I depending enough? Is Jesus truly living through me? Do I have enough works to show for it?" And maybe no other passage fuels this introspection more than James 2. For this reason, we should address the true context of the Bible's faith-works chapter. Is James really telling us to examine our Christian life's track record to determine if we're trusting? Should we self-examine to such a degree? Or is his landmark chapter really about something else altogether?

Throughout history, many have struggled with this passage. In fact, Martin Luther held that James shouldn't be part of the biblical canon because of the presence of this faith-works passage! Admittedly, it's not easy at first glance to reconcile the teaching of James 2 with the teachings of Romans, for instance, which state that we're justified by faith alone and not by works (Romans 3:28; 9:30–32).

James 2 clearly says we're justified by works too, not by faith alone. To dance around this passage by saying it refers to works after salvation is faulty. The passage specifically asks, "Can such faith save them?" (James 2:14). In addition, it repeatedly addresses the issue of becoming justified before God, a status that occurs at salvation. Without a doubt, James says we're justified by works and not by faith alone. But the important question is: What does James mean by "works"?

I believe the key to understanding this passage is to avoid bringing our twenty-first-century mind-set to the table, especially with regard to the term *works*. Rather than assuming that *works* should be understood as a lifelong record of religious activity, one should consult the biblical text and let the writer himself define the term. James's own use of the term *works* is quite different from how we use it today.

James explains that even demons can believe the basics of Christianity—that there is one God, and so forth (2:19). He shows us the difference between nodding your head with dead faith versus expressing living faith. The purpose of the passage is to communicate that faith without decision or response is dead faith.

> The purpose of James 2 is to communicate that faith without decision or response is dead faith.

James uses two Old Testament examples, Rahab and Abraham, to explain justification by works. Both characters actively responded to God's message. They didn't sit back passively and claim that they believed God. Rahab decided to open her door to the spies (Joshua 2:1), and Abraham chose to offer his son on the altar (Genesis 22:3). They went beyond mere intellectual assent and did something in response to God's message.

But how many times did Rahab open the door? Once. And how many times did Abraham hoist his son Isaac on the altar? Once. Hence, works in this passage is really *not* about a lifelong track record of good behavior. It's actually about the importance of responding to truth—an act that goes beyond intellectual agreement. James 2 might be summarized by the following train of thought:

- We're justified by works (but *works* needs to be defined in context).
- Works are like what Rahab and Abraham did.
- Living faith involves opening a door (of your life)—a work.
- Living faith involves offering someone (yourself)—a work.
- So living faith involves decision—a work.
- Any faith without decision is just dead faith.

James 2 communicates that personal decision is necessary in order for true salvation to occur. Those who appear to fall away from belief in Jesus are those who merely associated themselves with certain doctrines for whatever reason. They may abandon Christianity the movement. They may abandon Christians, sometimes accompanied by personal resentment. But they don't abandon Christ, since they never knew him. Ascribing to certain doctrines is one thing, but opening the door of your life and receiving the life of Christ is altogether different.

Once James 2 is seen in context, it doesn't conflict with Romans or any other faith-centered passage. We need to recognize that this passage in James does *not* seem to be referring to a post-salvation experience. It's specifically addressing the question, "Can such faith save them?" (James 2:14). From there, we must grasp James's own use of the term *works* by consulting the examples he gives. James's purpose is to contrast mere intellectual agreement with active, saving faith that involves receiving the life of Christ. When Christ stood at the door and knocked, did you respond by opening the door, as Rahab did? If so, I think you've met the "requirement" of this historically controversial faith-works passage.

> If you opened the door of your life, I think you've met the requirement of James 2.

James 2 is not inviting us to introspect and assess our long-term track record of good works; in context, it appears to be contrasting dead faith (intellectual assertion only) with living faith (true conviction followed by *decision*).

We must never forget that truth is supposed to set us *free*!

PART 7

ego assault

There is this kind of dangerous element about the true presentation of the doctrine of salvation.

D. Martyn Lloyd-Jones (1899 – 1981)

30

WHILE I WAS A PROFESSOR AT THE UNIVERSITY OF NOTRE DAME, WE lived in a three-bedroom home in downtown South Bend. Our two spare bedrooms served very specific purposes. One was for guests, and the other functioned as my office. We kept the guest room spotless, just in case. We never knew when we might have a last-minute guest. My office, on the other hand, was a complete wreck. Old books, papers, and equipment were strewn across the room. It was difficult to walk around in the room without stepping on trash.

Imagine you're walking down the hallway of our home. And let's say you're looking for a spot to throw something away. Where would you be more likely to toss your garbage? In the guest room? Or in my office? In my office, I suppose. Well, thanks. I appreciate that! No, I can understand why you'd choose my office. It's already full of trash anyway.

As you reflect on this scenario, let me ask you an important question: Which room are *you*—the dirty office or the spotless guest room? How do you see yourself? Your answers to these questions determine what you do with garbage that comes your way.

Picture a sinful thought traveling down the hallway of your mind. If you're the dirty office, then why not just add one more piece of trash to the pile? You're dirty anyway, so it doesn't really matter. But if you're the clean guest room, garbage doesn't seem to fit there. It's out of place.

Our standing as completely forgiven, righteous saints is given to us, before heaven, for a reason. It has everything to do with daily living. In the moment we're offered a sinful thought, how do we perceive ourselves? As dirty or clean? As sinful or righteous? As sinners or saints? If we're dirty sinners, then why not just place one more sin on the pile? But if our slate has been wiped clean and we're now righteous like Christ, then sin just doesn't fit.

It's out of place.

CLEAN FOR LIFE

Some are afraid the teaching of the New Covenant will somehow lead to more sinning. Nothing could be further from the truth.

> Some are afraid the teaching of the New will somehow lead to more sinning.

God himself has declared that awareness of our clean state is the way for behavior change to occur. In fact, anything other than this motivation for upright living isn't the gospel in action.

Below are two Bible passages that directly link knowledge of our forgiveness and new identity with daily behavior choices. It's easy to see that our beliefs about our spiritual state can directly affect our actions:

> Make every effort to add to your faith goodness; and to goodness, knowledge; and to knowledge, self-control; and to self-control, perseverance; and to perseverance, godliness; and to godliness, mutual affection; and to mutual affection, love. For if you possess these qualities in increasing measure, they will keep you from being

ineffective and unproductive in your knowledge of our Lord Jesus Christ. But if any of you do not have them, you are nearsighted and blind, and you have *forgotten that you have been cleansed from your past sins.*

2 PETER 1:5–9, italics added

Those who listen to the word but do not do what it says are like people who look at their faces in a mirror and, after looking at themselves, go away and immediately *forget what they look like.*

JAMES 1:23–24, italics added

What are we really afraid of when it comes to believing in our clean, righteous state that is not obtained daily through confession or request? Do we really believe it will lead to more sinning? What's the difference between sinning first and then asking for forgiveness versus being forgiven already and then sinning? Is the former somehow more humble or more spiritual?

The reality is that the amount of time we spend sinning won't increase if we agree with God about his Son's once-for-all sacrifice. In fact, the opposite will occur. We'll begin to realize that our slate is clean before God. We'll see that Jesus Christ accomplished this in order to remain in us every moment of every day, no matter what. With awareness of his unconditional presence comes the power to say no to sin.

In Ephesians, Paul also addresses the attitude of forgiving and releasing others from anything they've done. His reasoning is that it's the same treatment we received from our heavenly Father: "Be kind and compassionate to one another, forgiving each other, just as in Christ God forgave you" (Ephesians 4:32). Essentially, Paul is saying "Pass it on!"

Since we've already examined our once-for-all forgiveness in Christ, this passage can mean a lot more. As a blanket statement, God has declared that he keeps no record of our wrongs. We can't begin to pay him back. He has released us from what we owe him, even if we continue to do the same things over and over again. If we never realize what we've done, or even if we forget about our sins altogether, we're still forgiven.

Our own forgiveness isn't contingent on our memory, our sorrow, or our apology. It rests solely on what was accomplished at Calvary. This is the amazing forgiveness that God *chose* for us through the finished work of his Son.

> We can issue the same blanket statement to others: "You're off the hook!"

In light of this all-encompassing forgiveness, Paul urges us to allow our hearts to be softened and to issue the same blanket statement to others: "You're off the hook!" We can *choose* to release others just as God released us, even if they *never* realize what they've done and even if they do it *again*. Do you see how an understanding of our once-for-all forgiveness is essential to releasing others with no strings attached?

THE SELF ISSUE

But it's not just our forgiveness that leads to good behavior. Paul also makes a direct connection between *identity* and behavior:

> Do not lie to each other, since you have taken off your old self with its practices and have put on the new self, which is being renewed in knowledge in the image of its Creator.
>
> COLOSSIANS 3:9–10

This is just one example of how crucial it is to be aware of our new identity in Christ. People tell lies to protect themselves or delay pain—or for other self-edifying reasons. With an unshakable identity and all of our needs met in Christ, we're not designed to live in fear. So here we see a bit of divine logic applied to the behavior issue: "Don't lie *because you're a new creation.*"

Here's another example. These verses give us insight into what should motivate our expressions of forgiveness and grace toward others:

> As God's chosen people, holy and dearly loved, clothe yourselves with compassion, kindness, humility, gentleness and patience. Bear with each other and forgive one another if any of you have a grievance against someone. Forgive as the Lord forgave you.
>
> COLOSSIANS 3:12–14

Paul first affirms our true identity. Then he acknowledges that we have a choice to put on one thing or another. He urges us to "wear" qualities that match who we are and how God treats us.

The phrase *clothe yourselves* speaks of getting dressed spiritually. Paul is essentially asking, "What will you wear today?" Just as we wake up every morning and choose the outfit we'll wear, we also choose what to put on spiritually.

Does this sound like oppressive religion to you? It's not in the least! Paul is simply appealing to our God-given common sense to suggest healthy choices. The outcome of indulging the flesh can be stressful and divisive. But living from our new identity leads to peace, fulfillment, and unity.

BEHAVIOR VERSES

Behavior follows on the heels of the New. It certainly does not act as a condition for it. We forgive because we're already forgiven. We release others because we've already been released. We see others as God sees them because we too have been made new as a gift.

Behavior passages foretell our destiny. It makes sense to seek them out and crave them, since they quench our thirst for conformity to Jesus Christ. They're a road map for saving time and expressing who we really are. And as we live out who we really are, we experience peace:

> Neither circumcision nor uncircumcision means anything; *what counts is the new creation.* Peace and mercy to all who follow *this rule*—to the Israel of God.
>
> GALATIANS 6:15–16, italics added

We can concoct all kinds of doctrines and motivations for upright living. But the only thing that really matters is the new creation. And as we focus on our newness and Christ's presence within us, our behavior changes.

Nearly two thousand years ago, the apostle Paul penned thousands of words begging the church to leave the law behind, to make central the finished work of Christ, and to discover who they really were. And I believe he'd have a similar admonition for the church today:

Behavior follows on the heels of the New.

> *Celebrate the New!*
> *Learn who you really are!*
> *And then just be yourself!*

31

I WAS PETRIFIED AT THE THOUGHT OF GETTING MARRIED. KATHARINE and I had been friends for four years, and then we dated for a year and a half. She was beautiful, intelligent, and sincere in her desire to know God in a deeper way. We had a lot of fun together too!

My reservations really didn't have anything to do with Katharine. I was just so afraid of making a mistake that I could hardly move forward in the relationship. But one night I drummed up the nerve to propose to her, and we were engaged.

As the wedding approached, I grew more and more tense. At one point, I informed her, "I'll be at the altar, but I may be on a stretcher." Romantic, huh? I didn't know how I was going to make it.

The day of the wedding was the worst. My anxiety level was so high that I nearly turned around and ran out of the church. I wanted to marry Katharine, but I could hardly breathe!

After the ceremony, I wasn't really sure what I was feeling. But the next morning, I woke up and felt a strange peace. All of a sudden, the emotions that'd been so strongly negative were gone. In the coming months and years, I've watched our marriage relationship grow strong and flourish. God was with us for sure.

His Will

Why all the anxiety and stress before the wedding then? Again, it had nothing at all to do with Katharine. I was so wrapped up in whether or not I was in God's will that I could hardly move. In fact, this had happened repeatedly with various dating relationships throughout my early adulthood. I would freeze up and not know what to do. I'd pray for answers, but God never seemed to tell me anything.

I had grown up with a heavy emphasis on finding God's will. I was taught that God has a perfect will and a permissive will. God's perfect will is like the bull's-eye on a target, whereas his permissive will is like the outer rings of the target. Ending up in his permissive will would only yield a second-rate experience. Our goal is to stay in the bull's-eye—his perfect will. How do we do that? Well, we just have to follow his direction. How will we know what he wants us to do? Just listen. And if you can't hear him, you're just not listening hard enough. Or maybe you're deaf to his voice because of the sins in your life.

Needless to say, this view of God's will paralyzes those who adhere to it, because *God is not interested in controlling our every move.* Nor is he sending us secret messages about what decisions to make if only we'll listen hard enough. Because I had fallen victim to error regarding God's will, I was like a deer in the headlights when one of life's major decisions—marriage—came at me.

> This view of God's will paralyzes.

Having gone through such a stressful decision-making process, I was determined to find out the truth about the will of God. As I consulted Scripture, I discovered that the will of God boils down to the following:

- that none perish but all believe
  (1 Timothy 2:4; 2 Peter 3:9)

- that salvation come to the Jews *and* Gentiles
  (Ephesians 1:5–2:22)
- that we present our bodies to him every day
  (Romans 12:1–2)
- that we bear much fruit
  (John 15:8; Colossians 1:9–12)
- that we pray throughout our lives
  (1 Thessalonians 5:16–18)

God's will is essentially that Christ live *in us* and express himself *through us* as we are *transparent* before him.

The scriptural view of God's will turned out to be dramatically different from what I had heard. This put an end to my perpetual wondering about whether or not I was "in God's will" with regard to daily decision making.

In discovering that God's will is *Christ in me and Christ through me*, I could see that God was behind every door, even the door of sin. I'm not saying that sinning is OK or that God wants us to sin. Of course not! What I mean is that whether or not I choose a particular door in life, God will always be there. He will be there because he's in me. He's not just *with* me, but he's *in* me. So wherever I go, there he is!

Fear of Freedom

Freedom to choose can be a scary thing. It means that displaying passivity as I wait on God to *decide for me* doesn't make any sense. It means being responsible and learning from consequences. Most important, it means going through life without secret messages that lead to safe, successful choices all the time. Ultimately, this means there's an air of mystery about the future. Although the inaccurate view of God's will is appealing to the flesh, there's nothing like living and growing under the freedom to choose.

As I contemplated the stress I had experienced over getting married, I noticed that the apostle Paul himself expressed his freedom concerning marriage, stating this about himself and his fellow apostles: "Don't we have the right to take a believing wife along with us?" (1 Corinthians 9:5). Although Paul was free to choose any believing woman, we know what he ultimately decided. After surveying all possibilities, he decided it was best to remain single. This was most likely due to the distress in the early church. After all, is it an act of love to marry a woman when you know you'll likely be martyred soon? So, although Paul had freedom to marry any believing woman, he employed some God-given common sense and decided not to.

> Many Christians are paralyzed as they wait for God to tell them which car they should buy, which house they should purchase, or whom they should marry.

My point is that many Christians are paralyzed as they wait for God to tell them which car they should buy, which house they should purchase, or whom they should marry. This framework for decision making appears to be very spiritual, but it's not scriptural.

FROM THE HEART

When we come to the realization that we're new creations with new hearts and new minds, we can live as God intended. We can wake up every day and ask, "What do I *want* to do?" and "What makes the most sense?" We can trust that if it is not motivated by fleshly appetites, it is sanctified by the very fact that a new creation is doing it. We're free to live from our wants, since we, together with our hearts, minds, hobbies, and interests, are now set apart in everything we do.

This is freedom! Scary? Maybe. But we're in a much better position if we live from what's actually biblical rather than what we *feel* God is like. As we move toward maturity and thank God that we can learn from our past choices, we experience Jesus, who will never leave us or forsake us.

So what do you do when you've pondered and even prayed for wisdom, but God isn't deciding for you? The bottom line regarding tough decisions is to learn your new identity in Christ, live from your heart *and* mind, and enjoy life!

You don't have to succumb to the paralysis of analysis. Christ is in you, and you are in Christ.

So God is behind every door!

32

MY WIFE, KATHARINE, IS QUITE THE WOMAN — A SUPPORTIVE wife, a great mother, a research scientist, and a sailboat captain. On one of her overnight sailing expeditions to the Bahamas, Katharine encountered life-threatening circumstances. Together with a few friends, she found herself moored on a coral reef in the open water a long way from any other boats or land. Katharine was an experienced sailor, but she made one potentially fatal error. She read the tide charts in the opposite way such that low tide was misunderstood as high tide.

As the sailboat sat on top of the reef, the water grew rougher, and the vessel keeled sideways in the wind. A couple of her friends hopped over the side and swam under the boat to see how badly the coral had bitten into the hull. Would the boat be diced to pieces? Was it possible to drag the boat off the coral without serious damage to it? After some investigation, they believed the boat's hull to be intact, but there seemed to be no way to remove the vessel from its wedged position.

The only solution was to wait it out. For hours they sat there until high tide rolled in and rescued them from the reef. You can imagine the relief they experienced as they finally reached the harbor in the Bahamas — dry land, hot showers, and good food. Arriving at their final destination meant so much more to them given the obstacles they encountered on their way.

Katharine's misreading of the tide charts led to a stressful predicament with no safe harbor in sight. Christians today can experience something similar without an accurate understanding of the New Covenant. I'm not talking here about logging time reading words on a page. Katharine did that with the charts! The problem is that she misread the charts and arrived at the *wrong meaning*. In the same way, we may feel we know what the Word says, but do we really know what it means and what it means for us personally? I've met some knowledgeable Bible scholars who were filled with anxiety and had no "safe harbor" in their lives.

In Hebrews 4, we're told of a Sabbath-rest, a safe harbor for the people of God. Upon entering his rest, we rest from our own works, just as God did after creation. This safe harbor is a spiritual attitude we adopt because of the finished work of Christ. The resurrection enables us to relax in a protected place—to rest easy, knowing that we're secure, accepted, forgiven, and righteous. When the low tide of law living threatens to entangle us in a reef of sin, we can refer to the "charts" again. A proper understanding of the New Covenant will allow us to find safe harbor.

This book has been about my own misreading of the charts and how I, and others like me, have found safe harbor. Remember the REVEAL survey I referred to in chapter 2, which showed that more than a quarter of maturing Christians were stagnant or dissatisfied with their spiritual lives? But it's nearly impossible to be dissatisfied once you've encountered the truth in all its life-changing power. My prayer is that you, like so many others, will reap benefits from the stripping down of all the convoluted ideas we've added to the message over the years—from the truth laid bare, from the *naked* gospel.

> A proper understanding of the New will allow us to find safe harbor.

"ALL GONE"

I've tried to make the naked gospel as transparent and easy to understand as it is in Scripture. The real gospel should be easily understood by young and old, educated and uneducated. After all, it was successfully delivered to thousands of people by fishermen of no particular status or educational background.

Understanding the real thing should not require a new and extrabiblical vocabulary. Just as a child knows the meaning of "all gone" at the end of a good meal, God has simply and emphatically proclaimed to his children:

- Your relationship to the law is now *all gone*.
- Your old self is now *all gone*.
- Your sins are now *all gone*.
- All obstacles preventing closeness are now *all gone*.

It's amazing how simple and straightforward the naked gospel really is. In fact, most of my exposure to the New has involved more *un*learning than learning. Once we remove the clutter from our theological closet, the gospel shines brightly again. And it once again becomes a powerful, practical benefit to us on a moment-by-moment basis.

If it's the real thing, it will change lives radically, but it will also bring controversy. Wherever the real gospel is taught, it results in false accusations of many kinds. Consider John, for instance, who found himself having to clarify that the gospel promotes *upright* living, even though we *still* sin:

> My dear children, I write this to you *so that you will not sin*. But if anybody does sin, we have an advocate with the Father—Jesus Christ, the Righteous One.
>
> 1 JOHN 2:1, italics added

Similarly, we find Paul responding to accusation as he answers the frequently asked question "Shall we go on sinning so that grace may increase?" with these words: "By no means! We are those who have died to sin; how can we live in it any longer?" (Romans 6:1–2). Obviously, some had accused Paul of teaching that it was OK to use our freedom for sin (Romans 3:8; Galatians 5:13).

Grace, in your face, begs questions. Grace, in your face, brings accusation. Nevertheless grace, with no condition to ruin it, must be taught without regard for the reaction. Given the radical nature of the genuine message, these words of D. Martyn Lloyd-Jones may point us to the litmus test for any preaching we choose to sit under:

> There is no better test as to whether a man is really preaching the New Testament gospel of salvation than this, that some people might misunderstand it and misinterpret it to mean that it really amounts to this, that because you are saved by grace alone it does not matter at all what you do; you can go on sinning as much as you like because it will redound all the more to the glory of grace. *If my preaching and presentation of the gospel of salvation does not expose it to that misunderstanding, then it is not the gospel....* There is this kind of dangerous element about the true presentation of the doctrine of salvation.
>
> D. MARTYN LLOYD-JONES, *The New Man:*
> *An Exposition of [Romans] Chapter 6*
> (London: Banner of Truth, 1972), 8–9, italics added.

As we put forgiveness, freedom, identity, and new life side by side, we encounter a gospel that at first glance appears dangerous. But upon further examination, we discover just how brilliant our God is in designing a bulletproof covenant that brings *real* relationship and *real* change into our lives.

BULLETPROOF MESSAGE

When some worry that once-for-all forgiveness with no strings attached will lead to more sinning, we can assure them that God was not naive in making such a move through the cross. On Calvary, God also dealt with our core desire to sin. In Christ, we have died to sin and don't really want it anymore. Conversely, when others have only grasped their new identity in Christ and then fail to meet their own unrealistic expectations concerning performance, we can comfort them with the truth of once-for-all forgiveness.

> We discover just how brilliant our God is in designing a bulletproof covenant

When some feel they have already gained an intellectual grasp of forgiveness and identity but still lack the "power" to make any real change occur in their lives, we can remind them of the life of Christ they possess—his presence and his power over sin. Conversely, if others have already come to know a life of dependency on the risen Christ but still get tripped up by how much they're *not* doing or *not* giving, we can rescue them from measuring themselves through a reminder of our freedom from a law system.

In short, the real gospel is a bulletproof message that is essentially spiritual common sense from every angle. It makes biblical and practical sense, and there is no verse in the entirety of the Scriptures that ruins its splendor.

Think about it. If it's the genuine historical message that God has always intended for us, then every passage in the Bible must eventually fall into place in light of the most powerful, overarching truths.

ALIVE AGAIN!

"My Bible has come alive again for me. Words leap off the page like never before, and I can actually understand what I'm reading for the first time." Over the years, I've heard statements like this countless times. And isn't that what it's all about? Being counseled by our own personal Counselor as we dive deeply into his Word? And once we become aware of the reality of the New Covenant, things become a lot clearer.

So have you been awakened to how good we have it on this side of the cross?

If so, there's really only one sensible thing to do.

Thank God.

nude reflections

PART 1:
obsessive-Christianity disorder

1. In what ways do you think hitting rock bottom better prepares you to grasp the true meaning of the gospel?

2. Are there areas in your life where you feel you may have hit rock bottom? If so, what may God be trying to tell you, if anything?

3. Why do you think so many experienced churchgoers are stagnant and stalled? What do you feel they are missing?

PART 2:
religion is a headache

1. Who is your favorite Old Testament character? Had you ever imagined that you have a better relationship with God than they enjoyed? How might realizing this concept affect your daily life?

2. What is God trying to communicate to you today by the fact that Jesus was born into the tribe of Judah rather than into the law's priestly line of Levi and Aaron?

3. As you think of Hebrews 7:18, how has the idea of law-based living been "weak and useless" in your own life? Are there ways in which you need to agree that the law has been "set aside"?

4. The New is simple and straightforward, but even the early church struggled with adding conditions to it. How do we add conditions to it today?

5. A common misconception is that God writes the law of Moses on Christians' hearts. What's wrong with this view? How would you clarify the issue for someone?

6. If a friend were to say to you, "I know I'm not under the law, but we still need rules and Christian principles to guide our behavior," how would you respond to that notion?

7. What are your hesitations about abandoning "the law" as a system and fully trusting in God's new way?

PART 3:
crossing the line

1. Had you ever thought about how the New begins at Jesus' death instead of at his birth? How might this impact your view of Jesus as he taught his fellow Jews?

2. How might a new understanding of the dividing line between the Old and New Covenants affect your study of the Bible?

3. How have you been doing with regard to Jesus' teachings of "gouge out your eye and cut off your hand in your fight against sin," "be perfect," and "sell everything you have"? How does understanding the cross as the great divider between Old and New help you identify Jesus' purpose in these teachings?

PART 4:
burning matryoshkas

1. What does it mean to you that Christ is your life? How is this different than Christ merely being a *part* of your life?

2. What might a Christian conclude if they believe they have a "sinful nature" as opposed to struggling with the flesh?

3. How does the power of sin masquerade as you in your life?

4. How does an understanding of the presence of sin make you *more* responsible for your actions?

5. What would you say to someone who thinks that recognizing the power of sin is shifting the blame by insinuating that "the Devil made me do it"?

6. Do you think this is all just semantics? If not, how do you think an understanding of the flesh, the power of sin, and your true identity in Christ can be a practical help in a normal, everyday situation?

PART 5:
cheating on Jesus

1. How do you sometimes show a lack of confidence in the "once for all" nature of your forgiveness?

2. Even some world-class seminaries refer to the "atoning death of Christ" in their doctrinal statements. But how does the Old Testament term *atonement* (meaning "covering") fall short?

3. How does the image of Christ your Priest *seated* at God's right hand impact your perspective on how God views you?

4. The idea that asking for forgiveness is not biblical is new to some Christians. In your opinion, how are asking and thanking different? What makes thanking God for forgiveness more in line with Scripture?

5. What benefit is there in confessing your sins to another person? How might this practice be misunderstood, misused, or even abused?

6. How does an accurate perspective on 1 John 1:9 keep us from cluttering up the issue of once-for-all forgiveness?

7. If fear of judgment or expectation of rewards is not supposed to be our motivation for daily living, what should provide the greatest motivation?

8. What do you perceive to be the difference between conviction and counsel? How does knowing the difference help someone who is plagued with guilt and condemning thoughts?

PART 6:
we don't marry dead people

1. Why do you think it is important to understand the meaning of Jesus' death *and* his resurrection?

2. How might knowing that you already have everything you need for godly living affect your daily life? Your prayer life? Your relationship with others?

3. Is the mystery of "Christ in you" difficult to fathom? How would it change your perspective on your life's meaning and purpose to know that Christ literally dwells within you just beneath your skin and bones?

4. How does a "saved by Christ's life" perspective influence your understanding of eternal security for believers?

5. What would you say to someone who was hesitant, or even fearful, to surrender his or her daily life to Christ?

6. The Bible tells us to continue to live our lives in Christ in the same way we received Christ as Lord (Colossians 2:6). What was your attitude in receiving Christ as Lord? How is it similar to the attitude you can have as you live your life in him?

PART 7:
ego assault

1. How do you think a solid understanding of the New Covenant will impact your attitudes and behavior on a daily basis?

2. Which of the two main reasons to avoid sin do you believe could be most effective in your life—because we are not designed for sin, or because there are consequences to sin?

3. Return to the quiz on pages 27–28. Review each item carefully. Are you now able to discern why each quiz item is false?

4. Of everything God has granted us through the New Covenant, what means the most to you personally? How might it affect your relationship with God in the long term?

5. The New Covenant message is radical and powerful yet surprisingly simple. Why do you think it's not taught more clearly in churches today?

sidebar

Sidelight 1 *(from page 62):* **Fulfilling the law is something that God *did* in Christ.** Its fulfillment isn't an ongoing event in the lives of believers today. God set us free from the law, so that we're not under it or supervised by it (Galatians 3:25).

The Holy Spirit isn't motivating us to keep the Mosaic law, nor do I think we should consult the law as our guide for daily living. This is why we have the Holy Spirit in us instead: "But if you are led by the Spirit, you are not under the law" (Galatians 5:18). Furthermore, if God were motivating us to adhere to the law, it would be the entire law, not part of it. Imagine what the Holy Spirit's tutelage would be like if he were motivating us to obey hundreds of Mosaic regulations.

I believe it's quite clear that believers should have *no relationship* with the law. Romans 7 explains that we've died to the law, and we're now married to Another. God views a return to law-based living as spiritual adultery. Living by rules is cheating on Jesus!

Sidelight 2 *(from page 73):* **The fruit of the Spirit is a beautiful phenomenon.** The expression of Christ far exceeds any human notions of morality or ethics. In the garden of Eden, Adam and Eve made the mistake of choosing to "know" right and wrong.

They entered the realm of morality and ethics in which they could judge good and evil. Rather than living from the Life that gave them breath, they chose *control*.

The original sin didn't outwardly appear to be evil, nor would it be ridiculed today. It might even be praised today, just as we applaud those who seek what is "right" in their own estimation. We call it integrity and self-discipline. But God wasn't pleased with the first humans' decision to enter the realm of right and wrong.

God intended us to be dependent on him with no concern for morality and ethics. Adam and Eve were only to know this: the life I display is God's life. With that, they were to be satisfied. But the story of the fall is that they weren't satisfied. They were tempted to settle for a substitute. That substitute is something we call morality and ethics today.

Where does this leave *us*? Christ lives in us for the same reason that God gave life to Adam—so we can be dependent on Christ with no regard for any other means of living. As Adam could once say, and as the apostle Paul stated, we also can now say: "I no longer live, but Christ lives in me" (Galatians 2:20).

If we get life from the Spirit, then we're not designed to live by the Jewish law, religious rules, a moral code, or even Christian "principles." Receiving and transmitting Christ's life is superior to them all.

Sidelight 3 (from page 80): As Galatians informs us, Jesus was born under law. As Hebrews tells us, the Old wasn't replaced by the New until Jesus' *death*. Therefore, the gospels are a history of Jesus' interactions with Jews *before* the New goes into effect. Any belief system that doesn't take this into account will leave a Christian bewildered. Trying to mix Jesus' teachings directed to Pharisees and zealous Jews with the epistles will inevitably result in confusion.

Jesus tells his audience to cut off their hands, to pluck out their eyes, and to be perfect just like God. He tells them that their righteousness must compete and win against the Pharisees'. He says that they must first forgive others in order to be forgiven. In short, Jesus is *discouraging* his contemporaries as they seek to achieve righteousness through the law. He does this so that he can later grant them perfect righteousness as a gift through his death and resurrection.

Sidelight 4 (*from page 80*)*:* Acts is not a series of doctrines designed to instruct the church on daily living. Instead, it's a history book detailing the apostles' travels and the impact God had on the early church.

So where might we go wrong by using it to form doctrines? As examples, one might erroneously arrive at these doctrines by relying on events in Acts: (1) when a person believes unto salvation, they should expect a tongue of fire to descend on them; (2) if a person lies about how much income they are setting aside for the church, they may end up falling dead; and (3) speaking in foreign human languages is immediately exercised on salvation. Although these events occurred in Acts, it doesn't mean they should be taught as *doctrine.*

The early church era was a time of transition. God was performing wonders in order to announce that Yahweh could now be found through the person of Jesus Christ. Imagine the momentum it would take to present an entirely new covenant to those who had experienced the Old for so long. Likewise, God moved in powerful ways to initiate his gospel among the Gentiles who had no prior covenant at all.

The sparks that flew in the early church were something special to behold. To expect them today *with the same intensity* will certainly result in disappointment. That level of display is simply not needed. We now have a written record of God's Word that has been translated into many languages of the world. The message has now spread nearly worldwide. In many places (though not all), teachers of the gospel are welcomed with open arms. This certainly wasn't the case in the first-century church.

I'm *not* saying that any spiritual gifts have been extinguished from use. I'm merely making the point that one shouldn't expect to form doctrines broadly applicable to all Christians from the historical events in Acts.

Sidelight 5 *(from page 92):* Taking the Ten Commandments away from a believer can be spiritually akin to taking a safety blanket away from a child. The child may feel insecure, but removing the crutch is essential to helping them become mature. It's natural for adults to feel insecure when something we've seen as a foundation for our lives is figuratively yanked from us. But realizing our release from the law is an essential step toward Christian maturity. The apostle Paul minces no words in making freedom clear to the first-century church and to us today.

The law was never intended to serve as a foundation for the Christian life. We have no right or scriptural basis by which to select portions of the Mosaic law and claim that these should supervise believers. Paul teaches that believers are led by the Spirit and are not under the law. Thus, even the Ten Commandments are not designed to guide our daily living. The Ten Commandments are described as a ministry of condemnation that brings death. Who wants that in their life? We're also informed that sin gains an opportunity through commandments, including the "Big Ten." The law causes sin to increase, not decrease. Therefore, we can expect *more* struggle and *more* sinning if we adopt the law as our guide for living. Conversely, our release from the law directly results in a release from sin's power. Apart from law, sin is dead.

But we shouldn't ignore the purpose of the law today. The law is holy and perfect, and it has a particular use in the world today.

It's designed to convict sinners of their depraved state. It shows the dirt on the face of humanity, but it can't offer a solution. Only Jesus Christ cleanses us from the sin that the law reveals.

Although the law plays an important role in the world today, it has no place in the life of a believer. The Spirit living in us is God's superior replacement for the work of the law. In fact, what the law couldn't do in its inferiority, Christ has already done through placing us in perfect standing before God. Our calling is to break free from the law and cling to the Spirit alone as our guide for daily living.

Sidelight 6 (from page 119): If a surgeon were to cut your body open on an OR table, of course they would *not* find the power of sin inside! In the same way that we can't visually locate our spirit or soul, the power of sin is also invisible. Every day it busily delivers messages to us.

Just as Jesus was tempted with thoughts, the world and sin itself tug at us by appealing to our five senses. Receiving sinful thoughts from a third party is no indication of your own nature or true desires. In recognizing the power of sin operating through the body, we can account for temptation, yet still understand that we're new. We can agree with God that the old self is gone and that our struggle isn't against ourselves.

Sidelight 7 (from page 122): Believers still sin, but *not* because of the old self. The old self has been crucified and buried with Christ. If you're now in Christ, the spiritual person you used to be has been obliterated. The new you has been raised and seated with Christ. You're an entirely new creation, and there's nothing sinful about the core of your being. Your righteous human spirit is where Christ lives.

Some expository teaching on Romans dances around the reality of our crucifixion with Christ. The reason that some hesitate to come right out and say that our old self has been obliterated is that we still sin. We feel it'd be hypocritical to teach that the old self has been removed when we ourselves still struggle with sin. But the apostle Paul was no hypocrite, and he provides us with two solid reasons for why we still sin.

The first is the presence of sin, a power that lives in us but is not us. The power of sin is not the old self. The power of sin *controlled* the old self. The old self was a slave to sin, while the new self is not. Likewise, the flesh is not the old self either. The flesh is all of the programming (mind-sets, attitudes, reactions) that builds up over time as a person allows sin to operate in his or her life. When we're made new in Christ, those memory banks of how to cope with life are still in the brain. We can still resort to walking according to the flesh.

So the old self has been annihilated, but two interdependent operators are still at work to sway the believer toward unbelief. This is why we still sin. If expositors would teach the presence of sin and the flesh alongside the teaching of our old self as crucified, buried, and gone, they wouldn't need to worry about anyone presuming that they teach the heresy of sinless perfection.

Sidelight 8 (from page 123): Some use Paul's statement to the Corinthians, "I die daily" (1 Corinthians 15:31 NASB), as fuel for the die-to-self theology. But in context, *this passage has nothing to do with the old self and the new self.* Instead, it is simply Paul's defense of his apostleship. He is merely saying that he puts his life at risk on a daily basis, even encountering wild beasts in Ephesus. He is obviously referring to the *physical* dangers he has encountered. This is no basis for a die-to-self theology.

In Matthew 16:24, Jesus says, "If anyone wishes to come after Me, he must deny himself, and take up his cross and follow Me" (NASB). This verse is indeed an invitation to lose one's life. And this is precisely what happens to Christians *at salvation.* We lose our former life as we are crucified with Christ (Romans 6:6; Galatians 2:20). So for a Christian to go on trying to continue to "die to self" is to ignore the exchange of the old self for the new self that took place at salvation.

The bottom line is that Christians don't need to die to self. Instead, we need to grow in our awareness of who we are at the core. In this way, we walk according to the Spirit and not according to the flesh.

Sidelight 9 (from page 125): "It's just semantics" is a response I often hear when presenting the truth about our new self and why we still struggle with sin. Actually, it's not! A Christian who thinks they still sin because of the old self is fundamentally misled about their nature, their true desires, and what the work of the cross accomplished. The bottom line is that we're not fighting against ourselves. This is significant, since Jesus taught that a house divided against itself will not stand.

The truth of our identity in Christ has very practical applications. When we say no to sin, we're *not* saying no to ourselves. When we reject sin and choose to express Christ, we're living out our destiny and fulfilling our deepest desires. Although the flesh is ugly and sinful, we aren't. Although the power of sin is crafty, devious, and sinful, we aren't. We're clean, and our hearts crave what God desires for us.

Sidelight 10 (from page 165): I am aware that at first glance Hebrews 6 and 10 also appear to communicate either judgment or potential for loss of salvation for the believer. I will address both passages thoroughly in my upcoming book centered on Hebrews. Here I will simply note that the author of Hebrews is addressing "enemies of God" who tasted the rain of the gospel falling on them but did not drink it in. They kept on sinning by committing the only sin mentioned in the first ten chapters of Hebrews—the sin of unbelief in the gospel. No other type of sinning is brought up in the epistle before these warnings are issued. From the context, it is evident that the author is addressing those who currently teeter on the fence, while true believers are "not of those who shrink back" (Hebrews 10:39).

acknowledgments

I WANT TO ACKNOWLEDGE MY WIFE KATHARINE. WITHOUT HER support and encouraging feedback, this book would not have seen the light of day. Thank you, Katharine. I love you!

I want to recognize my mother, Leslie Farley. The fact that she was open to her heavenly Father enabled me to get a taste of the real thing early on. I am grateful for the grace-filled home that she fostered while I was growing up.

I would like to acknowledge the leadership of Ecclesia. Their support and encouragement was indispensable as I completed this book. In particular, I want to thank Rex Kennedy for his encouragement to me over the years and Chip Polk for his fiery zeal to communicate this message through Ragtown Gospel Theater.

I want to recognize Rob Jackson of Extra Credit Projects for his creative talent in designing the cover. And a special thanks goes to Beth Jusino of Alive Communications.

At Zondervan, I want to thank Andy Meisenheimer for making this book *so* much better. In addition, I am grateful to Dirk Buursma and Beth Shagene for their attention to detail and thoughtfulness in copyediting and in designing the interior. I also want to thank Maureen Girkins, Dudley Delffs, Ginia Hairston, Tom Dean, Mike Salisbury, Robin Geelhoed, and Jackie Aldridge for partnering with me. My experience with them has been amazing, and I couldn't ask for a more supportive publishing house.

Share Your Thoughts

With the Author: Your comments will be forwarded to
the author when you send them to *zauthor@zondervan.com*.

With Zondervan: Submit your review of this book
by writing to *zreview@zondervan.com*.

Free Online Resources at
www.zondervan.com

Zondervan AuthorTracker: Be notified whenever your favorite
authors publish new books, go on tour, or post an update
about what's happening in their lives at www.zondervan.com/
authortracker.

Daily Bible Verses and Devotions: Enrich your life with daily
Bible verses or devotions that help you start every morning
focused on God. Visit www.zondervan.com/newsletters.

Free Email Publications: Sign up for newsletters on Christian
living, academic resources, church ministry, fiction, children's
resources, and more. Visit www.zondervan.com/newsletters.

Zondervan Bible Search: Find and compare Bible passages in
a variety of translations at www.zondervanbiblesearch.com.

Other Benefits: Register yourself to receive online benefits
like coupons and special offers, or to participate in research.

ZONDERVAN®

ZONDERVAN.com/
AUTHORTRACKER
follow your favorite authors